Far more than a captivating story of a <del>rock</del> <del>....</del> *the reason why he is passionate for everyone to experience peace and a life of purpose regardless of how stuck or hopeless they may be. Many answers to life's questions can be found on these pages confirmed by evidences of a changed life in a man called Rob.*

Lloyd Hoover, *Bishop Overseer,*
Lancaster Mennonite Conference Network of Churches

A compelling story of redemption, forgiveness and healing, Rob's journey gives hope to anyone struggling with addiction, loss and crippling rejection. Once a remodeler of houses, he has now become a remodeler of lives. Rob's supernatural conversion to Christ in a jail cell came with a passionate vision for rescuing the broken and afflicted. His story from captivity to destiny will inspire the reader to reach for God's love and freedom.

Ron & Mary Buch, *Senior Pastors, Breakout Ministries, Leola, PA*

I've been privileged to watch Rob live his life and observe the changes God has made. I have worked beside him in the administration of The Potter's House, and have witnessed life changes in the men God touches through him.

Jay Mylin, *Board Chairman of The Potter's House Ministry*

In reading this book you will find inspiration, hope and encouragement that will rapture your heart.

Pastor Craig Snow, *healing and deliverance ministry*

A
RAPTURED
HEART

ROBERT M WEATHERHOLTZ

A Raptured Heart
by Robert M Weatherholtz

Published by
Weather-All Publishing
Brownstown, Pennsylvania
Rob@arapturedheart.com

ISBN: 978-0-578-34670-0

Unless otherwise noted, all scripture quotations in this publication are taken from the *Holy Bible, New International Version* (NIV). © 1973, 1978, 1984 by International Bible Society. Used by permission of Zondervan Publishing House. All rights reserved.

DEDICATION

This book is dedicated to
my Lord and Savior Jesus Christ

To my loving wife Beth
and our children Jacob, Joshua, Jonathan and Tecia

To all those who labor in the field of addiction and recovery
counseling as well as healing and deliverance ministry,
Your work is not in vain!

This book is written in memory of my daughter, Jessica, who
lost the battle with addiction. The pain of losing her fills my heart
with passion to lead others out of the darkness of addiction
and into the freedom of Christ. I miss you, sweetheart!

ACKNOWLEDGEMENTS

I want to first of all thank my loving wife, Beth, who sacrificed close to a year of Saturdays as I wrote this manuscript. Thank you for believing in me!.

Thank you to my sons Jacob, Joshua and Jonathan and my daughter, Tecia, who, having seen the best and the worst in me, have shown unconditional love. I am proud of you and I love you dearly.

Thank you to The Potter's House Ministry Board of Directors and staff for believing in me and the vision for the Still Waters Recovery Center.

Thank you to all of the pastors, churches, counselors, recovery groups and financial supporters who desire to bring healing to those who have suffered the impact of brokenness and addiction. May you be blessed!

Thank you to the Chaplaincy at Lancaster County Prison: Bud Roda, Ron Buch and all who labor in this field.

Thank you to my writing team: Sarah Sauder, Diane Omondi, Debbie Mllette, Katie Noit and Lanny Millette. Without their help this book would not be a reality!

CONTENTS

INTRODUCTION

Life can take many twists and turns. It may leave us in places from which we may feel there is no way out. Confused, broken, and with nowhere to turn, we lose hope for a meaningful life. Beaten by circumstances, we are unable to make sense of why we were given life at all. We can find ourselves lost in a vain pursuit for our identity and alone in the quest for answers.

I am not the only person to experience hopeless despair. Millions are trying to make sense of life. They begin with purpose, intending to walk a good path and live out their dreams. Then one day, life takes a turn and spirals out of control. One set of devastating circumstances follows another. Problems mount up and the disappointments accumulate. They search for anything that will numb reality—and get sucked into a lifestyle that they never intended to be in.

Have you ever felt this way? That is my story. Lost home, lost family, lost career, thrown in prison and shut out from the world. within four walls of a dark, dingy prison cell. How did I end up here? What went wrong? The pit of despair seems too deep to climb out.

Can you relate? Day after day passes. Every night when the lights go out, you find yourself all alone in a place you thought you would never be. Tormenting thoughts of "if only's" are your companion. Then morning comes and you awaken to another series of dogs barking and guards with little compassion for your basic requests. *You have reached your breaking point!*

Awesome! Now we are ready for the Master's Hand! It is in that very time of our breaking that we come to the end of ourselves. And that, my dear friends, is when ***God shows up***! When we have exhausted all human reasoning we come to the end of ourselves. That is exactly where the Lord meets us.

Let's go on a journey together down a road of redemption, birthed out of the fires of adversity. A journey of childhood dreams turned into the trials of a broken family. A story of a man trying to do family the right way.

My story is a testament to God's ability to supernaturally heal the human heart and raise up a warrior forged into a caring man of passion for the healing of broken human hearts. A man consumed by a fire to help others find their way out into wholeness and grafted into their destiny as a child of the living God through a personal relationship with His Son, Jesus.

May this story grip your heart as you delight in the true story of a redeemed life and the impact it can make on the world.

Robert M. Weatherholtz
Associate Ministry Director
The Potter's House Ministry at Still Waters
Pastor of Addiction, Recovery and Discipleship

CHAPTER ONE

Wait a Minute!
It's Not Supposed to be this Way!

I began life in the small town of Middletown, Pennsylvania, along the Susquehanna River. In my earliest memories my parents were always shouting and fighting. Chaos was ongoing, with few moments of any real peace, clarity or reason. The turmoil and drama never seemed to end.

I am the youngest of seven children. An older brother left home and joined the army the year after I was born and an older sister ran away to Florida with an older man to escape the madness of growing up in our home. My dear mother forged out a living for five of us kids as best as she could in those days. She was a hairdresser and ran her beauty salon in our home to save money. Saturday mornings, I usually woke up to a bunch of ladies laughing in the front room of our house and the distinct smell of perm solution in the air. Yukko! I have fond memories of my mother packing us all up and taking us to French Creek State Park. Sometimes, if we were lucky, we made a trip to Ocean City, Maryland.

My father was a truck driver and a Korean War Veteran. Being around him was a militant experience to put it mildly. He was an angry man and very abusive to my mother and my sisters as we were growing up. While I could not understand him as a child or young man, I was able to understand why he became that way much later in my life.

I have bittersweet memories of those days. My father would bring me really cool bicycles and we were one of the only families in our town to have an in-ground pool. To the public eye we looked like an average American family living out the American dream. But it was a completely different story when my dad would come back from a cross country trucking trip and stop at the local tavern before coming home.

When I was about four or five years old, my dad came home one night really drunk. He began screaming at my mother. She was no match for his aggressive behavior and his brute strength. When she demanded that he leave, I saw him punch her in the face and knock her to the floor. He sat on top of her and began to pound on her. My sisters came running to try to protect her, but he just pushed them away and threatened to beat them if they didn't stop interfering. Children should never have to witness this kind of atrocity, especially in a family where they are supposed to feel safe and protected. One of my sisters ran out the door to call the police. While he chased after her, I took the chance to climb on top of my mom and sprawl my body over hers. I cried out, "Please stop hurting my mommy!"

When my dad returned, he found me laying on top of my mom. He stopped the beating. The police showed up at our house. After a struggle, they handcuffed my dad and hauled him away for quite some time. My mother had to go to the hospital for several days. My whole body was maxed out with adrenaline. I remember the embarrassment I felt when the news of what happened got around town. I had nightmares and the fear and trauma carried through into most of my adolescent, teen, and young adult years.

How does a young child cope with that much trauma? My perception of the sanctity of family was being formed throughout this tragic experience. But this was only the beginning. We ended up moving from town to town trying to stay away from my dad, but he would always track us down. When he would find us, it just meant more trauma and more arrests.

One Christmas Eve when we were living in a redwood cottage several blocks from the Susquehanna River, my dad showed up again. He glared in the front window and all I could see was evil in his eyes. Petrified, my sisters and I ran to the back bedroom and hid for fear of what he might do if he got in. When my mom refused to let him in, he picked up my bicycle threatening to throw it through the sliding glass door in the front of the cottage. My mom screamed that she was calling the police. He ran away and didn't come around for some time.

By the time I started elementary school, we had moved to Elizabethtown, Pennsylvania. The trauma stopped for a while. I began to make friends and when I was eight, I got involved in sports—baseball to be exact. I began to have some hope for a normal childhood and a chance for a better life.

How I loved the sport! But sometimes my dad would show up at my games. He would stand in the crowd flashing money, prodding me to hit a home run. This embarrassed me terribly in front of my coaches and the whole community. Many times, I did not even want to come out of the dugout when I knew he was there. It was so humiliating.

Several times they stopped our Little League games so that my coach could ask my dad to either be quiet or leave. My coaches used to come by my house to check on me as they knew the trauma that our family had been through. They showed an interest in me and treated me as a young man with a lot of potential. I think this attention from baseball coaches marked the first time in my life that I felt loved and genuinely cared for. I went on to win several league championships and was selected as Most Valuable Player twice. I had three no-hitters as a "southpaw" pitcher throughout my baseball career.

When I was ten years old, my dad showed up again on Christmas Eve at our house in Elizabethtown. My mom ran him out of the house because he was roaring drunk. From my hiding place in her beauty salon, I watched him out the front window stopping traffic on Main Street with a bottle of whiskey in his hand. He was offering Christmas drinks to everyone who drove by. Once again, I felt the shame of living in a dysfunctional family with a father who was a monster. How could he not see the damage he brought to our family?

Later that evening we were notified that he went to a bar on the outskirts of town. When they refused to serve him because he was drunk, he smashed his bottle on the counter and slashed the owner's face with the broken glass. Of course, this was in the newspaper. We were the talk of the town once again. How could this happen in a different town where I was making a good name for myself? I began to resent my father deeply. I was angry that while other families seemed normal, mine was crazy and out of control most of the time!

The man who was supposed to protect me instead traumatized our whole family! Why couldn't he just leave us alone, I wondered. Where was God in this? Why was my family such a mess while everyone else's seemed to be normal? Who was going to protect us from this horrible atrocity I knew as my dad? How was I supposed to understand the fundamentals of life when my father was a walking, talking time bomb looking for a place to go off? That was the example I had to learn from about being a father and relating as a son.

My dad reunited with his childhood sweetheart. From the time I was 10 until I was 16, they lived in Texas. It was a relief to be free of the war zone that came with having him in our lives. It was during this time that I began to escape into alcohol and marijuana. The first person to offer me pot was my Little League baseball coach. I was 12 and wanted the affirmation of older males. Along with the drug culture came teenage sexual behaviors with young girls. I was looking for love even though I didn't know what love was. I just wanted to feel loved and be normal. With the substance, I could make all the things that were bothering me go away even if only for a short time. I thought I had found the perfect escape. I could forget the trauma and feel like I was accepted if I had a drink or smoked some weed. I could numb the harshness of my reality and, in some way, feel some relief.

Without a father figure around, I began to run wild. I was rebellious and out of control throughout most of my teens. I got involved with the druggies and lived a life of anarchy. I was arrested several times and placed on probation for destroying public property and stealing money out of milk boxes. A bunch of us around fifteen years old set a dumpster on fire while drunk and smoking weed one night. I can't even explain why I became so rebellious apart from the fact that I traveled with a bunch of like-minded, wounded, fatherless kids and we wanted attention at any cost, even if we had to set the world on fire to get it. We felt neglected, abandoned and rejected by our fathers and the world that we grew up in.

This marked the beginning of many years of upheaval and strife in my life, I experienced along with deep trust issues with male figures and deep-seated unforgiveness.

Look at this story and gaze into a great chasm of decay in the fabric of our society. We are all responsible to care for those who are brought up being abused. We need to learn to recognize when we are seeing it and then do our part to help children whose hearts are being shattered in broken families. We can't just turn a blind eye to them and what that pain produces in the form of broken men and women.

I pray that our judicial system, government agencies, counselors, prison officials, churches, and law enforcement agencies would take the time to look beyond the behaviors and realize that, for the most part, the individuals who commit offenses were not born criminals. They did not choose to be raised in a war zone without proper role models or godly instruction from parents. They did not have the privilege of a stable environment in which they could grasp healthy fundamentals for growing into responsible, authentic men and women.

Incarceration should be used as a last resort in dealing with men and women that have deeply wounded hearts. Prison will never heal the wounded heart. Most of the time it will only serve to harden these hearts and create generational brokenness for countless generations going forward. We need to take a good, hard look at how to heal these wounded hearts and arrest the cycles of brokenness that are being perpetuated in many diverse ethnic groups and backgrounds. Families that are seemingly whole cover up the things that go on behind closed doors so that the world will never see what is really going on.

Galatians 5:1 states, "It is for freedom that Christ has set us free. Stand firm, then, and do not let yourselves be burdened by a yoke of slavery." This and other verses I will refer to can teach us so much. The Word of God verifies and establishes solid ground for the integrity and the posture from which this book is written.

Back to my story. The nightmare continued. At age sixteen, my mother allowed me to set up a music room in the basement of our apartment on Market Street. I had a state-of-the-art 8-track stereo, blacklights with wild posters on the walls, and a drum set that I would use to pound out my frustrations instead of running around getting in trouble. I believe it was my mother's way of trying to cope with the disparity she knew we had been exposed to as children. She wanted to provide a controlled atmosphere in which we could get wild and express our individuality. My mom would let my friends sleep over and would even buy us beer so we wouldn't go run around and get in trouble.

It was during that time that I became sexually active and ended up getting a girl pregnant. We were both seventeen and not nearly mature enough to raise a child on our own. We named our daughter Jessica. The girl's parents did not want me in her life at that time, so our relationship ended there. As she grew older, Jessica's mother sought me out and I was privileged to establish a relationship with my daughter. Jessica and I grew to love and care for one another a great deal as the years went by.

One of the most emotionally hurtful times of my life came when I was in my basement recreation room and I heard someone coming down the steps. I looked up and there stood my dad who I hadn't seen since I was ten years old. He came up to me and looked me straight in the eye and said, "Can anybody tell me where Rob is?" I was crushed! I hadn't seen this man in six years, and now he didn't even know who I was. At first, I said, "No, I haven't seen him." As he turned to walk away, I blurted out, "Dad, it's me, Rob." I started to tear up.

He looked at me in surprise and said, "Hello son. You sure have grown." As I regained my composure, we began a conversation with some small talk. He was telling me all about his adventures in Texas and did not once ask me how I felt about him being gone all those years or say with any sincerity that he had missed me. Where was the empathy for my feelings? How could he act as if it were no big thing that it been six years since we had spoken face to face?

I had really mixed emotions about my dad being back and wondered whether things were going to get any better. Every son has a deep yearning to affirmed by his father, even if that person is not the best example of what a father should be. At that time, I wanted a dad like all the other kids. I was young enough to try to forgive the past in hopes that it could open the door to establish a relationship with him. I told him that I missed him and hoped to see him again soon.

For a short period of time, I felt he actually tried to be a dad. I was glad to have him back in my life. But that did not last long. In the summer of my sixteenth year, he came up to our house and asked my mother to step into the kitchen to talk. I heard them yelling and screaming at each other. Memories of my childhood came rushing back into my mind. I had to run. I had to get away from this insanity! I told myself that I was going to run away! So, I grabbed a few belongings and slipped out the back door. I went to a friend's house who had often talked about running away to his grandparents' place out in Ohio. I told him that I was ready to make the escape, but that we had to hide out until my parents stopped looking around town for me. I spent a week in the woods behind the water company in Elizabethtown. I would sneak over to my friend's house at night to take a shower, then return to the woods to hide.

At that point, anything would have been better than returning to that house and being stuck in the middle of the yelling and screaming and fighting! I was just not going to have any more of it. I hoped to leave for Ohio that weekend with my friend and start a new life free from the insanity of my childhood. We were set to leave on Saturday night. An older female friend of ours that knew our dilemma was willing to help make the arrangements.

When the time came for her to pick us up, I came out of the woods and hopped into the back seat of her car. Out of nowhere a hand came through the window, grabbed me by the hair and pulled me through the window! It was my dad! He started yelling, "There you are you little drug addict! I'll show you how they deal with druggies in New York." He picked me up over his head and slammed me down on his knee! Crunch! I felt my ribs crack. He kept on pulling out handfuls of hair from my head and screaming: "You will never make your mother be worried sick about you again!"

I was terrified and in terrible pain! I wanted to kill him! He took me back to my mother's house. When my mother saw how I was walking, holding my ribs, and noticed that I had been crying, she freaked out. She started screaming at my dad telling him that he should be arrested. She was saying that she had told him not to lay a finger on me, only to help find her son. He stormed out of the house yelling obscenities about how ungrateful she was. I didn't see him again for quite a while.

I was in shock. It took me hours to stop trembling. I went to sit in a hot tub and soak my ribs. I remember taking off my shirt and seeing that my side was all black and blue. It was painful to even breathe. It took the rest of the summer to heal from that injury. Though I didn't see my dad during that time, I once again fell into depression and started doing harder drugs in an attempt to escape the reality of the hell that I felt trapped in.

I got into cocaine and barbiturates and drank heavily on top of it! I became an alcoholic at the age of sixteen. I would do anything to escape the painful memories, or at least suppress them. This became a lifestyle for me that lasted into my twenties. I withdrew into myself and created an imaginary safe place where no one could hurt me and I didn't have to be afraid.

I want to stop briefly and share some startling facts about most people who drink to the point of alcoholism. When a person first picks up a drink, it gives him or her a brief sense of euphoria. But with someone who has been traumatized, that euphoria becomes a place of escape. In a short time, he or she is unable to stop after a drink or two like a normal person. After the first drink or drug the brain chemistry is altered and the phenomenon of craving kicks off. The brain tells the body that more is needed in order to feel right. However, "feeling right" never comes; it just creates an illusion that "one more" will be the magic number. "If I just have one more, then I'll feel better." But better never comes.

Eventually that individual will drink to the point of destructive health consequences or begin to experience societal or legal consequences for obsessive drinking. What can't quite be understood by society today or even many medical or psychological counselors is why an individual would continue a destructive pattern of behavior knowing that it will lead to adverse consequences. What causes this out-of-control behavior to continue? "What sorrow for those who get up early in the morning looking for a drink of alcohol and spend long evenings drinking wine to make themselves flaming drunk." (Isaiah 5:11, NLT).

This is known as the obsession of alcoholism. It is sad for the individual as well as for the family of the person who gets caught up in the cycle of addiction. Be it drugs or alcohol, eating, or sexual sin, to the rational human mind it seems that there is a defect in that person's character. Mainstream religious communities might say they are just "rebellious". Either way, it is a malady that is hard to explain and challenging to diagnose, treat or correct. An incredible amount of underlying pain motivates this destructive behavior.

There are some great recovery programs that have developed ways to help individuals who suffer from these maladies. These include 12-Step groups like Alcoholics Anonymous, Narcotics Anonymous, Celebrate Recovery, Drug and Alcohol Rehabilitation facilities, and many more. However, I would like to take a deeper look at the individual who is suffering from this phenomenon of craving and obsession which seems to doom them to a life of chaos and destruction.

The spiritual aspect is often overlooked, or perhaps merely added on to the diagnosis and treatment. Many approaches just look at the behaviors of the person and try to speak to that aspect. Others try to address mental thought patterns with the belief that the way to get someone to stop a certain behavior is to change the way they think. This is the psychological approach. Others try to use nutrition, good eating habits and physical fitness as the means to health and wholeness.

These are all very important facets of wellness, but methods based on conflict resolution or behavioral modification miss the mark. While these are aspects of the process, they are not the holistic solution. Statistics reveal the ineffectiveness of thirty-day rehabilitation programs and the recidivism rates of those who need to come back again and again. This goes on at a tremendous cost to insurance companies, government agencies, and society as a whole. These cycles continue on and on—until there is a change in the person's spiritual perception of him or herself.

The prison system and courts constantly filter people through the systems of justice, using crime and punishment as a way to control behavior, but still have insanely high recidivism rates. Complete recovery and the return to life without addictions are the exception and not the norm. Why? How are we failing as a society? Can we find better and more effective solutions? There are many opinions about how we can deal with the scourge of addiction.

Let's look at the biblical perspective. Genesis 1: 27 states, "So God created mankind in His own image, in the image of God he created them; male and female He created them." We were created in God's image and God's likeness. Wow! Could it be that easy? Could it be that returning to the original plan God had for us from the beginning could be the solution for all things? Why then do we complicate and deviate from the plan God had intended for man since creation? Instead, we analyze the thoughts and the behaviors of human beings and come up with man-created solutions to the wounds of a God-created world. What we really need to do is to teach people that they were originally created to be "in His image" and "in His likeness." We need to show people how to return to that one sovereign factual component of what we were created for in the first place! Selah.

As the story unfolds, we will see how this truth is profoundly woven into the very fabric of our lives, whether we choose to acknowledge or reject it. God created human beings and established parameters in which they can live in an orderly fashion, with His very own moral conduct as our guide for right and wrong. Those principles are irrefutable evidence of His sovereignty over mankind and all creation. When violated, there are consequences. Though He provided a path to redemption through the finished work of His Son on the cross, we need to humble ourselves and recognize the great sacrifice God made to reconcile us and the world to Himself.

As you might have noticed, I have not yet mentioned any connection to church life in my story. Here I was, seventeen years of age, full of anger and frustration and having very little guidance from a mother or father.

I graduated from high school by the skin of my teeth. I had lost all interest in pursuing a baseball career and fell deeper into my addictions. I took a job at a local construction business in Elizabethtown. Most of the older guys there were heavy drinkers and party animals. I excelled at my work and was promoted to the position of foreman within six months. I had a very good work ethic from the time I was young.

With my mom raising us children single-handedly and as several of my sisters had gotten married or left the area, I was expected to step up as the only male in the house. I delivered papers and worked in restaurants as a cook and dishwasher prior to getting out of school. What I earned helped my mom as I pitched in for some of the extras so we could all have a decent life.

Soon after turning eighteen, I met a girl and was attracted to her as she was to me. We ended up having a child together, a daughter. I was working in construction and making good money, so we planned to get married and start a family. But as time went on, I decided I had to get a grip on my drinking and drugging if I was to become a father. I decided to go see an Army recruiter in town and sign up for the military. My brother Nelson had gone into the Army when he was young and it seemed to have turned his life around, so I felt that would be a good plan for me also.

I thought that the army would help me develop discipline and get some training. I knew that my family couldn't afford to help me go to college or even a trade school at that time. I signed up and went to take my civil service test, which I passed well. I shared with my then fiancé that I wanted to take her to meet my Army recruiter and hopefully plan together on how we could get married as soon as I completed basic training. We could then move to wherever they had me stationed. Little did I know what was to unfold.

As the time for me to take my oath and become property of the United States Army grew closer, my dad called. He said he was happy with my decision and wanted us to go out and celebrate. I was sure this would make him proud of me, considering that he was an Army veteran. I thought that being in the army would put me in a place where he would respect me as a man. We went out that night to several bars and he provoked a fight between me and a guy at a local tavern. In order to protect him, I had to confront this guy and take him out. I had been in a martial arts class for over a year and had advanced to brown belt level. I was in good shape for the military.

It was late and we had to go back to his house in Brownstown, Pennsylvania. To avoid getting pulled over for drinking and driving I agreed to go stay at his place and go home in the morning. Back at his house, he changed very quickly. That all-too-familiar evil look in his eyes appeared. I suspect that the fight in the bar, together with the alcohol, kicked off a flashback of his time in Korea.

Soon after we were at his house, he disappeared for about ten minutes. I assumed that he gone to bed. All of the sudden he came into the kitchen flailing a gun around. He forced me into a corner, grabbed me by the shirt and got right in my face. "I want you to remember something boy. I brought you into this world and I can take you out!" he said. I will never forget the fear and the adrenaline I felt in that moment when I looked him in the eye. I felt that he may, in fact, take my life right then and there! I was in panic mode, but something inside of me had had enough and I was not going to fear him anymore!

I mustered out the words in sheer anger and I yelled "Go ahead. Shoot me! I spent my whole life in fear of you and I'm not afraid anymore. Do it! Go ahead and do it!"

I stared him down. Thirty seconds seemed like a lifetime as all the years of my short life flashed before my eyes. We had finally faced off for the first time and I really wasn't afraid to die. I just knew I would never allow myself to live in fear of him again. At the end of our face off he began to come to his senses. He let go of me and turned and walked away. My heart was pounding out of my chest; I felt it was going to burst. I truly didn't know if he would kill me in my sleep. I had to get out of there. I put on my shoes, ran out of his house in shorts and a t-shirt even though it was a cold November night, and started to hitchhike back to Elizabethtown.

I walked almost the entire eight miles to Lancaster before a police officer picked me up and asked me what I was doing walking along the highway at two o'clock in the morning. I told him that I had been in an argument with my father and left before it got out of control. Little did he know, but it had already been way out of control. He took me to the Mt. Joy exit, and I walked the rest of the way from there. I was exhausted when I got home. When I told my fiancé what had happened, she was really freaked out.

The next morning the doorbell rang. When I opened the door, there stood my dad. I wanted to launch out at him, but he acted like he didn't even remember the night before and calmly asked me if he could take me to breakfast. This was weird! I played it off and told him I had some things to get done before leaving the next week for basic training. As he turned and began to walk away, I asked him, "Do you remember what happened last night?" He said, "Yeah, I remember. You sure did take it to that guy at the bar." He didn't say a word about pulling a gun on me—it was as if it had not happened! Then he turned around and walked away.

My life was bizarre. It seemed like a never-ending saga of trauma and turmoil that had no rhyme or reason. I was clueless on how to straighten things out and was deep in despair. But this was only a preview of what was ahead.

A few days later I was about to pack my belongings and go take my oath of allegiance, then ship off to basic training. I was with my fiancé at her parents' place with our daughter when I got a call that rocked my world. A friend of ours told me, "Rob, I think you are a good guy. I just really think you should know what is going on. Your fiancé is having an affair with your army recruiter. They plan to get together as soon as you have gone to basic training. You need to know. I think way too much of you to see this happen to you."

I felt like I had just been gutted and my heart had been torn from my chest! How could this be? I had to find out, so I called my fiancé and confronted her. She admitted to the affair. I was devastated! My whole life and the plans I had made came crashing down on me. I felt so betrayed and so played by an official representing the US Army that I went to the recruiters' office to confront him. I walked right into the office and asked the other recruiter who was there at the time if he could leave us alone for a short time so we could have a conversation. Of course, my fiancé had contacted him already and he knew some sparks would fly, so he told the other officer to stay.

Instead of taking on two US Army recruiters, I just began to tell him that I knew what was going on behind my back and I felt that what he did was horrible conduct, very unbecoming of a United States Army recruiter. I added that I was going to contact his superiors and let them know about it. I said I did not want to be a part of the US Army if these were the ethics and standards that they upheld. Meanwhile, underneath it all, I wanted to launch out over his desk and take him to school for being such a jerk. I know now that this is not normal conduct for an officer in the military, who I have come to know and respect throughout my lifetime.

Needless to say, I ended my army career before it ever started. I promptly broke it off with my fiancé and didn't see or talk to her or my daughter for years to come. Words can't describe the depression and heartbreaking disappointment I felt, along with the sheer disbelief that something like this could even happen. With the absurdity of my childhood and the disappointments of my early adult years weighing on me, I began to be a loner. I didn't trust anyone, especially women. For a long time. I felt that I could not endure another day of my life as I knew it. I contemplated suicide many times. But I had heard from somewhere that a person could go to hell if they committed suicide; that's the only thing that kept me from carrying it out. I could not understand a God that would allow all these things to happen, but I didn't want an eternal future in hell either.

Quite frankly, at this point, I couldn't imagine that hell could have been much worse than the sum of my life's experiences. How could I stop this madness? How could I forget the extremely broken memories? Was there a way out of this horrible place of turmoil that I had been born into and I had begun to accept as normal? I loathed the past and had no real plan for the future. There had to be more to life than what I was experiencing.

I went on living the life of a loner for quite some time. My drinking and rebellion against the world as I knew it became worse and worse. I got arrested a few times for underage drinking in my late teens and had to pay some fines. I became hard hearted and angry toward life and everyone who tried to talk to me about it. I didn't trust people because everyone I had ever trusted had betrayed me in one way or another. My thoughts and emotions were a constant roller coaster. Coping with life became harder and harder.

Then came the icing on the cake. I was having a conversation with my mother and telling her how I was struggling to get my life under control, not having a clue how that was going to happen. She heard my heart and wanted to help, but did the one thing that I never expected. She explained that right before she got pregnant with me, she and my dad had split up and she had an affair with a man who made her feel loved and respected. Then she dropped the nuclear bomb on me and told me that the man who I thought was my father all my life was indeed not my father at all. When she realized she was pregnant, she took back her husband out of fear, thinking that if he knew the truth, he would kill us both.

I was blown away! How could she have allowed me to think that this abusive man I called Dad was in fact he was not my father. I think she intended to give me a measure of solace, but it instead caused a bigger void in my heart and robbed me of the trust I had in my mother. After all, she had lied to me all my life. How could I believe anything else she said? Who in the world was this other man and did he even know that he was my father? This news just created a deeper break from reality within me. The chasm of mistrust grew larger and larger.

This was not how life is supposed to be! There seemed to be a never-ending labyrinth of lies and deceit along with a soul-crushing reality that everything in my life was a lie! My birth was a lie. My childhood was a lie. My last name didn't even belong to me. The questions grew deeper and deeper. I thought I was going crazy more than a few times and that death would be a better alternative than living. Nothing made sense. No one could be trusted, not even my own parents! My fiancé had betrayed me, and I was estranged from my daughter. She was being raised by another man whom I held in utter contempt. There seemed to be no way out.

I became angry and bitter towards the people who had lied to me and betrayed me. I would go out and drink and try to start fights in the bars. Alcohol would turn the anger into rage and fuel the hole in my soul that I didn't know how to fill. The saying, "hurt people, hurt people" applied to me in every sense of the word. I got into hard rock music and was at war with the world. I had this feeling deep down inside that the world wanted to destroy me; I had to fight back or die. I felt I would never escape the darkness and emptiness. This is a very dangerous place to be in life.

One day I had what I thought to be a revelation. I would finally run away and leave all this pain and sorrow behind. Without telling anyone, I packed a backpack full of clothes and drained the thousand dollars out of my savings. I left my job, my family, and my life behind. I was going to find a new life and I had no idea where it was leading me. All I knew was that I had had enough. I needed a change.

CHAPTER TWO

The Great Escape

So, there I was: twenty-two years old, angry at the world and ready to drop my whole life and leave everything behind. With a backpack, a Walkman stereo and a thousand dollars, I set out on a search for the meaning of life. I got on the highway and put my thumb out. Forty-eight hours later I was on a beach in sunny Ft. Lauderdale, Florida. That's right, I hitch-hiked 1,150 miles to a place I had never been and forged out a life there. I left behind all the memories. For two full years, no one including my family knew where I had gone.

When I first arrived, I slept underneath I-95 bridges, on the beach, in parks and where the homeless hung out. I got work from a labor pool a couple of days a week. Because I had a good work ethic, this led to a full- time job as a paint and wallpaper installer. I was thrilled because my first job was in Port Everglades working on a private yacht and getting it ready for a scene in the TV series Miami Vice. It was a 110-foot yacht called "Night Crossing." We had three weeks to get the renovations done.

The yacht was amazing! It slept sixteen people and had an entertainment area in the hull with a lighted dance floor, gold panther statues and a bar and lounge area. The bedrooms all had built-in surround sound stereo systems. The bridge from where the captain commanded the vessel was amazing. I would fantasize about being on this ship at sea and cruising to Australia where I would meet some incredible people and live my life far from the pain and drudgery I had left behind. I was allowed to stay on the boat for the three weeks of the renovations. The contractor then said he would not have work for a while, so I had to find another job.

I had learned at that point in my life to roll with changes, so I thanked him for the opportunity to work on such a wonderful project and the rich experience of living on a yacht for a couple of weeks. We parted with some kind words, and I went back to the street until I landed a job detailing cars. A place like Ft. Lauderdale has some very wealthy people and I got to detail some very high-end vehicles. Clients would come in with Porsches, BMWs, Mercedes, Jaguars and all kinds of top-of-the-line cars. I would get to drive them around the complex we worked in. It was exciting to work on the cars of some very famous people.

We also had a separate bay for work vehicles and rental cars for Hertz, Avis, and Enterprise, but the big money was in the higher end vehicles. I had a few customers that would request I be the one to do the work, then give me hundred-dollar tips when they got their cars back. I could actually earn more money in tips than from my paycheck, so this was an incentive to stay. I did stay there for almost a year. I was able to save enough money to move into a little place of my own and for a while I felt like life was good. I was starting to feel some contentment. I could work all week and go to the beach every weekend, at peace with myself and having a sense of being guided from afar.

One day when I was at work, a crew of guys pulled in with a fleet of trucks to be detailed. I started some small talk with one of them named "Bear" who appeared to be the foreman. I asked him what they were doing. He began to explain that they had come from Tallahassee, Florida, and had a contract with Asplundh to clear the power lines going across Florida from Ft. Lauderdale to Naples. Wow! That was the entire distance from the east coast to the west coast of Florida. I was intrigued by what all they would see in the Everglades and thought it would be a really neat experience. I was handy with a chain saw from going to my dads' property and helping him trim trees over the years and thought that would be more manly work than what I was doing at the time.

After a couple of weeks, he handed me a card and offered me a position on one of his crews. The money was awesome because it was a prevailing wage job paying close to thirty dollars an hour, much more than I was used to making. I took him up on his offer because they stayed in Ft. Lauderdale and I could stay in my apartment. The adventure of that job was amazing and a bit scary as we would go out and arrive at a place in the middle of the Everglades at daybreak. That can be an eerie experience.

I was warned to fire up my chainsaw first thing every morning to scare off local wildlife. Some mornings we saw alligators and water moccasins. They can be deadly if you do not follow the instructions on how to handle them. We also saw panthers and scorpions. I realized that this was not a place to let your guard down, but we had a job to do. All the wildlife would disappear at the first sound of those chainsaws.

I loved the work, but the crew of guys were heavy drinkers and partiers on the weekends. South Florida was the cocaine capital of the US back in the 80s. I developed an addiction to crack cocaine and alcohol in a very serious sense of the word as the drugs were so cheap and so powerful down there. I really thought that I was living a good life because that's what was normal to me. I was beginning to recreate the same life I had tried to run away from. It didn't take long until things spiraled out of control and my addiction was taking a higher priority than my well-being or my career.

I began to grapple with the depths of my condition and experience some of the consequences of getting caught up in that lifestyle. I was arrested for being in a motel room with a couple of hookers and drug dealers and charged with pandering, which is white slavery. The arresting officers thought that I was a pimp. I had to laugh about their perception of me as I was really just a lost soul from Lancaster County, Pennsylvania, caught up in a world I didn't really understand. I was released after a weekend in Broward County Correctional Facility after I appeared before the judge who actually laughed at me because I was clueless as to what pandering meant. When I gave my excuse for being in the motel room, he looked at me and said that I must really be out of my element.

This was my first experience of being incarcerated. I was really shocked back into reality for a short time. However, due to my addiction would have it, I would find myself in similar situations quite often and spend a good deal of time in and out of the south Florida prison system. I gravitated to a life of selling drugs to support my own habits and had some life-threatening run-ins. There was a time that I found myself running with a couple of Lebanese restaurant owners from Michigan. We were going out to try to cop some cocaine from a local hot spot and the driver was driving a souped-up Camaro which was a muscle car in those days. As we pulled up to the spot, a bunch of Jamaicans ran up to the car and put their hands in the front passenger side window. They had handfuls of cocaine in their hands. As soon as the Lebanese driver saw the drugs, the driver nodded and the passenger smacked the hands of a few dealers. Drugs flew all over the car! The driver floored the pedal, and we went racing out of there while they were laughing hysterically about what they had just done. I was in the back seat and started yelling, "Get me out of here and let me out of this car!"

I immediately heard the sound of gunshots! The back window shattered, and glass came spilling all over me! A bullet had come whizzing through the back window. We were under fire! The muscle car was fast. We sped away with no loss of life or injury, but I had been shaking for hours and hours when they dropped me off. They gave me a handful of cocaine bags and told me I did a good job. Really? A good job? These guys almost got me killed. Needless to say, I never hung out with them again!

Later I went walking through a familiar neighborhood to get some recreational drugs. Just as I was about to pay the person I was buying from, I felt a two-by-four smash me in the back of head! I fell to the ground unconscious. When I eventually woke up, I realized I had been robbed! I knew that it was a two-by-four because when I came to it was laying a few feet from me with blood on it.

These are only a few examples of the troubles I faced while in south Florida. I certainly do not wish to glamorize that lifestyle as there is nothing glamorous about it. It is a very dangerous and unfruitful path. Yet when a person is caught up in this kind of lifestyle, he tends to re-create it in any environment. I started my journey trying to escape the pains of the past and make a fresh start. I now found myself in a life full of even more insanity and life-threatening situations than those I had tried to escape.

Life's experiences can become the most profound teachers. Why would a seemingly intelligent person who has very good intentions still make very bad decisions?

The environment we grow in shapes our character, perceptions, and responses to our experiences. A person might feel the need to run from traumatic circumstances. This "fight or flight response" is an automatic response to events that are perceived as traumatic or frightening. The symptomatic nervous system is activated by the event and triggers an acute stress response that prepares the mind and body to either fight or flee.

This survival instinct can repeat itself in the life of a traumatized individual until it seems normal. The problem with this learned response is that it may lead to irrational decisions without wise counsel or planning and can set the individual up for even deeper levels of unhealthy decision making. Such was the case with me. I ended up running into the face of ever-present danger and creating that scenario all over again in a different environment.

Geographical change will not lead a traumatized person into a better way of experiencing life. To be effective, change must be internally motivated. In reality, we take ourselves with us everywhere we go. The environment is not the catalyst that can bring about change. Our perception of our environment is the only catalyst that causes change from within our hearts and affects the way our minds process life.

A person can be reared in a perfectly safe environment, healthy according to all human perceptions, but may try to create their own reality to deal with the inner conflicts they are experiencing if they perceive the environment they are in as a threat to their safety and stability. The standard of measure for how individuals process trauma and circumstances are similar in every economic, social and cultural level of society. Each person has the ability to adapt and overcome all the trials and situations in his or her life effectively. Without this, there is no hope for living a healthy and prosperous life in this world.

Here is where one's spirituality becomes a vital part of their ability to experience transformation. Romans 12:1-2 (NIV) reads, "Therefore I urge you, brothers and sisters, in view of God's mercy, to offer your bodies as a living sacrifice, holy and pleasing to God –

this is your true and proper worship. Do not conform to the pattern of this world but be transformed by the renewing of your mind. Then you will be able to test and approve what God's will is – His good, pleasing and perfect will." The posture of worship is the point from which a human being can begin to understand his or her reason for being born. When identity in Christ begins to take hold, a person gains a totally fresh perspective and can learn to process life from a holistic frame of reference.

How can we be transformed by the renewing of our minds? First, we must admit to ourselves that our way of doing life has not been effective. We desperately need to look at life in a compellingly different light or we will go on to a bitter end trying to figure things out through a broken lens. Proverbs 4:23 states, "Keep your heart with all diligence for out of it flows the issues of life." We need to deal with issues from a higher level of understanding if we ever want to overcome the obstacles that constantly bombard us.

This is only the mere beginning of the processes of transformation that the Lord wishes to bring about as we move toward an overcoming life story. If we do not change our perceptions, we will never change our circumstances and are doomed to repeat our past.

A longing for transformation began to call me to search for higher meaning and purpose in life. This was the beginning of a search for more and a quest to understand who I was and Whose I was.

After another year or two in south Florida working for a few different roofing and construction companies, I felt that I was at another dead end. It seemed I would never be able to grow into the person that I really wanted to become. I lived there from 1982 until 1987 when I decided to return to Pennsylvania and see my mother and my family who I hadn't seen in years. I missed my sisters and my mother and some of the friends I had left behind. My mother was aging. She had been pleading with me to come home, but for years I resisted. Finally, I made the decision to leave the life in south Florida behind and go home to try to pick up the pieces of my broken past. I packed up my belongings and dropped them off at a Goodwill store, sold my car, and boarded a flight to Pennsylvania.

In my heart, I sensed that I was coming full circle. I wanted to try to reconcile some of my past that I had run from, such as my relationship with my daughter, family members, and my employer who I had walked out on years prior without an explanation. My old boss was a good influence and had tried to help me. He had even co-signed my first loan for a car. I appreciated him and all he had done. I proceeded to make my rounds and make those amends upon my arrival. It felt good to clean up my back yard and ask for forgiveness for some of the irrational things I had done.

I was shocked when a few of my old school friends reported hearing that I had been killed in Florida. In a way I had become a conflicting legend in my own hometown. I was suddenly there in the flesh. Many people were glad to see me and gave me a big welcome. I entered a brief period of peace I felt a sense of coming home in my spirit that I couldn't quite explain. It felt safe—and it felt good. If only it had lasted more than a season.

Here I was, twenty-seven years old. I had traveled to some far away port of call and experienced life on a completely different level. I was restless. I went to work for another exterior home improvement business. I was a tough guy in a tough trade and once again worked my way up the ladder very quickly. I found myself back in with a bunch of guys that liked to work hard and play even harder. Worse yet, I had a head full of south Florida in a small town like Elizabethtown, and that was not a good combination.

I started drinking heavily every weekend and going to Reading, Pennsylvania to get drugs. I would bring these back to Elizabethtown to sell. This was the double life I was accustomed to. I was trying to keep my life under control, but the evidence proved that I did not have anything under control.

One night, an old school friend and I decided to take a run to Reading in his little red Triumph Spitfire. We thought we were so cool. When we pulled into the projects in Reading, I locked my eyes on a guy who looked like he was open for business. He started walking toward the car and all of the sudden stopped and turned around. Before we could figure out what was going on, we heard this voice say, "Get out of the car and put your hands in the air!"

"Oh no," I thought "We are going to jail!" We immediately complied. As we stepped out, three undercover drug task force agents with guns on us told us to lean up against the car.

For some reason, they told my buddy to get back in the car, then they searched me. Since we had not picked anything up yet, they did not find anything but a couple of hundred dollars cash in my pocket. They told me to get back in the car and they pulled the keys. My friend was sweating bullets. He told me there was a loaded gun under the seat that I should grab and hide in case they searched the car. I grabbed the pistol and put it down my pants!

After I had secured the gun, the officers came up to the vehicle and asked my friend to step out of the car. They searched him as well. Then they asked us both to get out and they searched the car! I was scared to death that they would search me again but for some reason they didn't. After they had searched the car and didn't find anything, they asked what we were doing in that neighborhood. Before my friend could speak, the words came out of my mouth. "We were up here trying to get some recreational drugs, officer." The officers said because I told him the truth, they were going to let us go—but they never wanted to see us in that area again.

In a strange way the saying "The truth will set you free" was true. In hindsight, I shudder to think that if they had found that gun, it would have been an automatic five years in state prison. But instead, I walked away without even paying a fine. I began to realize that there was someone or something looking over my life and protecting me because I should have been shot or in prison or dead long before. Since I was still alive, I still had a chance to turn my life around.

It was about that time that I became willing to listen to my heart and ask for help. I sought out some friends who had gone through a drug and alcohol rehab program and asked for their help to get me into a program. In those days, one had to go into the hospital for detox and then be referred to a program from there. Here I was, thirty years old with a life of out-of-control behaviors and insane events. The only thing I wanted to do was stop the madness! I was humble and ready to try anything to make sense out of this journey called life and find the meaning for my existence. When I agreed to go, my friend dropped me off at St. Joseph's hospital in Lancaster.

I questioned why most of my friends were getting married and building houses. They had their lives in order. Why couldn't I get it? Was I destined to a life of turmoil? Was there hope for me? My life was like a hurricane that threatened any attempts at a peaceful existence. I left behind a path of destruction in everything I touched and tried to do. I had reached my bottom and there was no way to go but up.

From detox they sent me to Clare Center in Wrightsville, Pennsylvania. I began my journey into the most quiet and peaceful time in my life up to that point. They helped me to understand a lot about my addiction and what caused some of the behaviors. I started to realize that there was more to my story than that of a bad person. I was reacting to life out of past traumas. It was a real epiphany for me to realize that my alcohol and drug use was only a symptom of much more deeply rooted issues.

I completed a thirty-day program there and agreed to go to another program called the Gate House for Men for another ninety days. This was the beginning of a season of incredible healing and growth. After I completed the programs, I got heavily involved in service in the fellowship programs that are recommended for people coming out of addictions. These are part of my ongoing recovery to this very day. There are a lot of good programs out there that help countless individuals recover from deficits caused by instability and dysfunction in their backgrounds. But there is a component that has to become part of your journey, or you will always be dealing with the issues of life without discovering its meaning.

Romans 8: 31-39 says:

"What then shall we say in response to these things? If God is for us, who can be against us? He who did not spare His own son, but gave Him up for us all – how will He not also, along with Him, graciously give us all things? Who will bring any charge against those whom God has chosen? It is God Who justifies. Who then is the one who condemns? No one. Christ Jesus who died – more than that, who was raised to life – is at the right hand of God and is also interceding for us. Who shall separate us from the love of Christ? Shall trouble or hardship or persecution or famine or nakedness or danger or sword? As it is written: For your sake we face death all day long; we are considered as sheep to be slaughtered. No, in all these things we are more than conquerors through Him who loved us. For I am convinced that neither death nor life, neither angels or demons, neither the present nor the future, nor any powers in all creation will be able to separate us from the love of God that is in Christ Jesus our Lord."

CHAPTER THREE

The Reckoning:
A Season of Understanding Grace

As I began to find a place of rest for my weary soul, I began to read the Bible in a different light. I grasped the concept of a God who loved me so much that He was willing to give the prize possession of His affection to come to earth to find me and restore the relationship that had been lost for generations. I realized that my entire line of past generations was broken and stained by sin. He wanted to restore that lost relationship so much that He sent His Son to pay the penalty for all mankind's sins and thus destroy the works of the enemy. He came to totally purge me and all mankind from our shortcomings, forgive us, and restore us to a relationship with Him, established in righteousness and not in our brokenness.

Jesus paid the consequences that I deserved with His own life and through His shed blood restored all of mankind who choose to accept Him as their Savior. The revelation of this truth captured my heart. I began to fall in love with this God who rewrote the story of broken humanity and gave us His beauty instead of the ashes of our broken lives. I realized that He was a good Father, and that Jesus promises in His Word to never leave me nor forsake me. This truth continues to carry me until today.

Father God was there with me when I was a child. He was there when I was confused. He was there when my heart was broken. He was even there when I ran away – protecting me, guiding me home, and preparing the way before me. Even when I could not see His hand, it was always holding and guiding me.

After I had been in recovery for around two years and I was starting to go deeper in my relationship with the Lord, something happened that I had not planned for. I was visiting with my mother one day in her apartment complex and she told me that she had run into a girl that I had dated back in high school. This was a girl who had moved from the area just as I started to fall for her. She had come to the apartment complex to seek housing.

I remembered the feelings I had for her fifteen years before but shrugged it off and went about my life. Sometime later I stopped in at my mother's again and she made a point to tell me that this girl, Mary, was moving in. She encouraged me to stop and say hello since she had said she would be excited to see me.

About a week later I stopped at my mother's apartment again and saw a car there with Florida license plates. I assumed the car must belong to Mary. After visiting my mother, I walked out to my truck, wondering whether or not I should go to see her. After toying with the thought for several minutes, I decided to go for it. Just as I went down the steps toward her hallway, she came walking around the same corner and we ran smack into each other! I started to laugh, a bit embarrassed at having run into her. She was just as I had remembered her, only a bit more mature in her features. Soon after that we exchanged numbers and started talking often. In a way, I am glad that God let her move away back in those days because I was still going through so much inner turmoil that it would have been a disaster for both of us if we had gotten together when we were young. I believe God is the one who allowed things to go the way they did. After a month or two, we started dating. Nine months later, I asked her to marry me.

We got married in the summer of that year. Almost a year later to the day we were blessed with our oldest son, Jacob. We had always talked about starting a business. We were very motivated and in the prime of our lives. I had been clean and sober for over three years. She knew my background from when we were kids, so she understood how I ended up there. With a few prayers and a few thousand dollars, we bought some equipment, an old truck with built in utility boxes, and some ladders. We put an advertisement in the local newspaper. I never thought that the business would take off like it did. Within a year, we had more work than I could keep up with. I bought a second truck and hired some local guys to work for me.

Two years after Jacob was born, we welcomed our second son, Joshua. Our business continued to grow. I felt immensely blessed back in those days as we were invited to join the Lancaster Building Industry Association and the Elizabethtown Chamber of Commerce. Things were happening at a very rapid pace and I was enjoying the fruits of a prosperous business. We held weekly Bible studies for our employees and sub-contractors and took them on fishing trips at the end of every year to show our appreciation for all their hard work. Life was good.

We continued to grow as a family and as a business. About four years into the business, we did some work for a local real estate brokerage and became friends with several of their salespeople. We ended up purchasing a house on a ridge with a spectacular view outside of Elizabethtown. On a clear day, we could see Ski Round Top in York County and the Columbia, Wrightsville bridge, 15-20 miles away from our front yard.

Our home was an 80-foot stone rancher with two bedrooms and a fireplace. It also had an attached, enclosed garage that gave you the feeling of a sunken living room. It had a pellet stove in the office area for heat. It came with 2¼ acres of wooded lot. For sure, we thought that we had arrived.

We had outgrown our previous office/warehouse location and decided to move the business out to the country near our new residence. We rented a warehouse and within two years we had purchased some new Dodge Ram trucks and a few dump trailers. At the peak of our business, we had gross sales of 1.4 million dollars per year. It looked as if we would have a long and prosperous life full of growth and progress. We had up to eighteen men working for us as sub-contractors and employees. We were living the "American Dream."

There had never been a time in my life when I had felt so complete as an individual, a husband, and a father. I was secure in who I was becoming. Things moved well for a good eight years. We welcomed our third son, Jonathan into the family. We grew to the point that I thought it was time to launch into some light commercial work. A company I had worked with for years offered us the opportunity to build a large commercial warehouse roof in Lebanon, Pennsylvania.

I thought this would be the opportunity of a lifetime! We would make a large sum of money in about two months and pay the house down or pay the trucks off. This would take us huge strides forward toward financial independence. I accepted the job and we got started. We had cranes come out to boom the material up to us as the roof was four stories in the air. I was really excited. About two months into the project, we called the company to ask for the draw we were supposed to get at the half-way mark of the job. There was no reply. A week later, I called them again.

At this point I was starting to worry. What was going on and why were they not returning my calls? I had about $35,000 wrapped up in materials and labor and I needed to make good on my commitments. I decided to go to their office. I arrived to see a notice of bankruptcy on their door. The place was locked up!

My heart seemed to hit my shoes. I had a sinking feeling to the point of being sick. "How could this be happening to me?"

I raced to call an attorney and I stopped construction on the job immediately! How could I recoup these losses? Was there any way to hold this company liable? We went into litigation with them for a period of at least a year or more as we paid lawyers to go after money that was not there. This business was protected under the bankruptcy laws so there was little if any recourse for regaining the losses. I was a wreck! I had worked my tail off for the better part of a decade to build this life for me and my family. Now I was being wiped out and I couldn't do a thing about it!

I began crying out to God, asking Him why He would bring me this far only to smash my dreams and allow this business to go under. After all I had been through in my life, I found myself feeling abandoned by God once again. I had let my family down and the dreams I once had were being dismantled right before my very eyes. I felt helpless. We tried to pay off our suppliers, but were not catching up.

We sold some of our equipment to a carpenter friend who lived right up the street from us. In an effort to keep our home, we made a decision to sell an extra lot adjacent to our home where I had planned to build a warehouse. When they went to excavate, we learned that our septic drain field was dumping right into their basement. The seller of that lot had not disclosed to us the easement on the adjoining lot which was on a separate deed. It was illegal to deed it as a separate lot with the drain field crossing that property line. We had not even recovered from the first losses and now we had to pay another attorney to correct this situation and hold the seller liable for the septic drain field.

This was becoming a nightmare. As the issues compounded faster than they were resolved, I began to have migraine headaches due to the stress and I stopped going to recovery meetings. I had been clean and sober for close to a decade and had worked so hard to build this life just to watch it all fall apart. The financial burdens became too much for us and we were forced to file for bankruptcy as well. Neither my wife nor I wanted to admit it, but all this took its toll on our marriage. A year later we moved to a farmhouse outside of Elizabethtown and tried to keep the business going, but things were not the same.

Between the losses and the headaches, the stress was unbearable. I was referred to a doctor in Harrisburg who aligned my spine and told me that my shoulders were so tense that my muscles were constraining the blood flow to my brain causing the headaches. I remember the first time he aligned my spine. I got so dizzy from blood that was released back into my brain that I almost threw up.

When I was visiting the doctor monthly for these adjustments, the doctor prescribed Xanax for the anxiety. I was so naïve. I thought that because the doctor prescribed it, it was okay for me to take it. He did not know my background. Neither was he aware of how to treat a person with a substance abuse disorder. I became quite accustomed to taking the Xanax to relieve anxiety. This was affecting my drive and my ability to function at full capacity on jobs. After about six months I tried to stop it "cold turkey" and went into a terrible withdrawal. My arms and legs were twitching involuntarily, and my nervous system was going haywire!

After two days I was unable to function, so I checked back into the Clare Center in Lancaster. After my detox period, they suggested that I go to a place called New Perspectives in Lebanon, Pennsylvania. I followed the recommendation. I was going through incredible highs and lows in my thoughts and feelings. I really wanted to get well so I stayed for the full twenty-eight-day program. I left feeling a lot more capable of navigating life once again with a bit more stability than I had before. I folded up the remnants of my home improvement business and took a job with a modular home setting company that had work up and down the east coast from Connecticut to North Carolina.

From that time on I was gone anywhere from ninety to one hundred hours a week. We might set a home one day in Virginia and have to be in Long Island, New York the next day, then off to the New Jersey shore the next. Now in my forties, I started drinking on the road again after a long period of abstinence. I was making good money, so I kept working that job for a few years. But all that time on the road began to take its toll on me, on my family and on our marriage.

My kids were growing up, but I was missing their games and school events. I would come home on a Saturday so exhausted from the road that I didn't want to go out in the yard to play ball with them. All I wanted to do was eat, drink a few beers and catch up on sleep. I was running myself ragged. I didn't realize that my family wanted me, not the money I was providing. How could I not see what was happening to me or my family? My wife told me so many times that she just wanted a life of peace, not striving for the security the world had to offer. I was unable to see it. She was indeed right.

My only role model on how to be a husband and a father was an out-of-control, demanding and abusive father with a broken marriage. The accusation that I was neglecting my family brought me deep inner turmoil. I did not listen to the suggestions I was given on how to handle these prompts from my wife with her feelings that I was missing the mark as a father. I gradually began to realize that even though I had not been a mean, abusive father, I had still become the neglectful husband and father that I never wanted to be. In some ways, that was just as harmful. I did not know what to do.

It was all too much for me. Life on the road was taking a toll on my body as I would sleep half the night in the back of a king cab pick-up truck after driving. Even when I did sleep, it was never restful. I was miserable at my job and miserable at home. I was overworked, over-taxed and burning out fast. All I wanted was a way to return to some semblance of normalcy, but my life had none.

I finally began to see the destruction in my own family after four years on the road. At long last I stepped away from the position and went back into contracting on a much smaller basis. I didn't realize that it was already too late. My drinking, abandonment, weekends away, and perception of my wife's demands had already done the damage. My wife and I separated. I could not emotionally handle visiting my three sons only on the weekends and not being together as a family. I slipped into a deep depression and started to drink even more heavily.

It was not long after our separation that my life began to spiral out of control all over again. I ended up getting three DUIs' in two years and I was in and out of prison like a revolving nightmare. When in a prison cell, I received papers stating that I was not permitted to come home to my family. This crushed me. When I was released, I felt that running away again would be the only way to get relief from the fear and worry which was my existence. It made no sense, but I thought it had to be better than the feeling of being trapped with the demands that I felt no person on the planet could have managed without going mad.

I would get out of jail on parole and each time I would face the same horrible loneliness and overwhelming responsibilities with mounting depression. There appeared to be no way out. I was paying child support, fines and costs and had to pay my rent in the places I found to live, with very little to no money to keep myself going. I had no driver's license. This translates into mundane jobs with less pay.

The amount of pressure that is thrown on a person who comes out of jail and society's lack of concern for the reality of their financial or emotional condition is one of the biggest reasons for the recidivism rates in our prison systems. Roughly 80 percent of all people in the county jails today are there for parole violations brought on by not paying fines and costs, falling behind in child support, or hopelessness. There is little help from our judicial system outside of punishment. We need to look to the restoration of the broken individuals lives and families. We need to heal as a society and change our perspective on how to bring about change. Only God can do this work through the power of forgiveness represented to us by our Lord and Savior Jesus Christ and the finished work of the cross. This is where my story really begins.

During this time of grieving and depression, I was in a constant state of turmoil. Isolated from my wife and family, I felt like I was all alone in the world and that my life had no meaning or purpose. I thought many times of suicide as the enemy kept trying to fill my head with lies that I would never amount to anything and had no hope for redemption. I had lost too much. I was as a man in a sinking ship, desperate for a way out or a way back and without hope. Nothing in my life made sense anymore. The overwhelming feelings of loss and depression that had mounted upon me with a vengeance were damning.

There was a time that I was on parole and my wife stopped in for her child support at the efficiency apartment I had rented. A week before that I had received divorce papers in the mail again and I was crushed. I didn't believe in divorce. I had watched my family fall apart. All this was emotionally devastating to me. I was so angry and hurt that I ripped up the papers and threw them out my apartment window. I was frustrated at trying so hard and not being able to overcome those obstacles. When my wife asked me for the child support, I told her that I didn't have it and that I had to pay my rent. Due to rain, I had not made enough money that week to pay my rent and child support. She probably didn't mean to pressure me, but I felt so betrayed. This led to a physical altercation. I felt horrible, and will always regret that things had reached that point.

I knew the police were going to get involved. Because I was on parole, it would have meant automatic jail time. So, I packed a backpack and got a friend to take me to a motel for the night. I heard from a neighbor that the police had come to my apartment. I called a gentleman that I had done some work for and asked if I could come get the money instead of waiting for him to mail it to me. I cashed the check and hopped on a southbound bus. I had no destination in mind—just a fearful expectation of what would happen if I stayed in the area.

I ended up stepping off the bus in Norfolk, Virginia. This was another place I had never been in my life. My only plan was to get away. I felt like a man without a country and a stranger in a foreign land. After getting another motel room for the night I boarded a bus headed for Virginia Beach in the morning hoping to find some work there. Although my heart was torn and my family was behind me, I was not going back because the only thing back there was more prison time and a boatload of heartache. I had to find work.

Upon arriving in Virginia Beach, I got a cup of coffee at a local convenience store and waited to see if any construction crews would pull in. Sure enough, after thirty minutes or so, several trucks pulled in with loads of roofing gear. I approached one of the drivers, saying I had just gotten into town and was looking for work. He took my phone number and told me he would call me that night. He did call. I told him that I had years of experience in roofing, siding and windows so he started me the next day at a decent rate.

For the first week I would work all day and get dropped off at the beach where I would go shower on the Boardwalk then sleep outside in a quiet parking lot. It was neither a safe nor a good place to be, but I made it work. After two weeks I saved enough cash to get a small efficiency apartment two blocks from the beach. I worked with that company for a year until we were doing a job for a guy who was a retired Navy Seal. He saw the way I took charge of things and asked me if I had any military background. I explained that I did not, but that I had grown up with a father who was a Korean War veteran. I also explained that I had owned my own roofing company for years and loved to work.

John Hawley and I became good friends. He invited me out to dinner with him and a couple of his old Seal Team members. They told me that they had a lot of a real estate including a number of rentals and invited me to come on board and do jobs for them. They offered me more than what I was making at the roofing business, so I agreed to take the position. This required that I move to a part of Norfolk, Virginia called Ocean View. I was blessed with one of their rentals and a company van to drive for work. I felt as if I had been rescued and hope had been reborn. I will be forever grateful for the kindness that John showed me in the midst of everything I was going through.

I ended up staying in that area for four years and I became very close friends with my boss. I respected his service to our country and his views on family. He worked with several other retired members of his former Seal Team. These guys attacked the real estate market as if it were a beachhead in a foreign land. Soon I was working full time doing roofing and contracting work for them and working on property flips on the weekends. Working for these men for three years had a great impact on my ability to take responsibility and get things done. They helped me face my issues under the weight of a lot of trials.

I will forever honor and appreciate the brave men of the Navy Seals as I came to know and love several of them as brothers and mentors in my life. My boss loved me like a son, but also knew that I was harboring some unresolved issues. One day he had me over to his house. He sat me down and asked me sternly but lovingly "What are you running from, Rob? Every time I ask about your family or your past you shut down and avoid the conversation."

That is when I told him that I had unresolved charges back in Pennsylvania and that I would have to do some jail time if I went back there. He was very understanding and said that he would try to do some background searches and see if there was anything he could do to help me to resolve these issues.

I felt really cared for. It was the first time I had felt that way since the days when my little league baseball coaches would pull me aside and want to help me with my home and family issues. I hoped that things would get worked out. As I grew in my position, I moved into a house. This was the most awesome arrangement I ever had in my life. I was right on the fence line of Little Creek Amphibious Base in Norfolk, Virginia. I had battleships in my back yard that I could see from the fence. This was also the base where they trained Navy Seals. Several of them came to stay with me before they deployed to Iraq during that conflict. These men were a whole other breed of integrity and know-how. I learned so much just from being exposed to them for the years I was there.

During that period, I mustered up the courage to call my then still legally married wife. She and our children sounded very happy to hear from me. She brought them down to visit a couple of times and I ended up apologizing for the way things had gotten out of control. I explained that I never wanted anything like that to happen and that it was never her fault. I also apologized for how I left in the heat of the moment because I did not want to go back to jail. So, there we were, a broken family with a boatload of hurt and legal issues, trying to make sense of all that we had been through. At that point I was just so glad to see my sons again that all the problems didn't seem to matter. Even though I knew I needed to return home and face the music, I still hoped for things to be worked out and against all odds be able to stay in my position in Virginia Beach.

The last year I was there I received a call from my sister that my mom had begun to develop dementia. I felt so bad I wasn't there. I also got a call saying that my dad had a heart attack and was going to have open heart surgery. I was torn between staying where I had built a life and going back to face the life that I had left behind. Though I wanted to stay, I needed closure. I did not want my parents to pass without me being there. When I talked to my boss about it, he said that as much as he valued me as a brother and as much as I was an asset to his business, I needed to go home and face my past. I took his advice. I packed up and returned to Pennsylvania.

I was able to visit my mother regularly over a period of four months, and stopped in to see my dad, but also knew that I had to face the criminal justice system. One day I mustered the courage to go to the Lancaster police station and turn myself in. I had dreaded this day for four years—but here I was. I needed to come to terms with all I had run from and left behind.

Upon arrival at the police station, they looked up the warrant and the officers came out and handcuffed me and took me into custody. I sat in Lancaster County Prison for three months waiting to go to court for my parole violation. I hoped that I would be released and put back on probation when I went before the judge. That way I could continue to work and pay my child support and see my mother and children. But when they finally took me to see the judge, he sentenced me to the unexpired balance of my sentence with no parole because I had left the state. That translated into a year in prison! My life came to an abrupt halt right then and there.

My heart sank into the depths of my being as I was taken back to the prison. I went through a gamut of emotions until I hit rock bottom. I had run out of hope. I found some solace by talking to a couple of the chaplains at Lancaster County Prison and reading the Bible that had been given to me. As I reflected back over my life, I just couldn't grasp how I had gotten married, built a lucrative construction company, raised a family, and after thirteen years, lost it all. I sat lost and broken in prison serving what felt like a life sentence. Even though it was only a year, time passes very slow behind the bars of the prison cell. The clanging of steel gates and the sound of dogs barking is maddening.

I read the Bible from Genesis to Revelation and started over again. For at least six months I didn't do anything but read my Bible and books that I would request from the chaplain's office. Dr. David Hain offered a class called, "Addict to Disciple." I learned so much from his teaching and years later, we became good friends.

Three chaplains in particular were very influential during that time. Bud Roda, a volunteer chaplain, is a man of God who genuinely cares about broken and suffering humanity. Ron Buch, another volunteer chaplain, would come on to the work release block and give powerful, hope-filled messages about a God who cared. I will always cherish Al Huber was the man who led me to the Lord. He was a very soft spoken and caring man who taught me about a God who loved me so much that He gave his prize possession to come and die to take away my sins and failures in the person of Jesus Christ. Al explained that God wanted to save me and redeem my life.

This was a far cry from the God who I perceived as a punishing God who let my family fall apart and wanted to make me pay for all the wrongs I had done. Could I have been wrong? Could He have been there protecting me and directing my steps all this time? Could it be that He really did want to save me and redeem my life from all the past hurts and mistakes? Could He make all things new? Psalm 103:4 says, "The Lord Who redeems your life from the pit, Who crowns you with loving kindness and compassion."

Were all my trials part of His plan to lead me to this juncture of my life? Was this what had been missing? I wanted to know this God who was the redeemer of broken men and the restorer of lives. I began to experience an insatiable hunger for the things of God. I would sit for days and pray and seek Him with all my heart. I would soak in His presence. It was as if I was not even in this place of destitution. It seemed that somehow I was completely free and that nothing could separate me from this God of amazing love! It was crazy. I was in prison yet felt like I was completely and totally free and loved.

I fell in love with God in a prison cell. But that was just the beginning. There was such a profound difference in the way I began to perceive life. "How can a man find joy in the confines of a prison cell?" I wondered. "What is happening to me? Am I losing my mind or is this real?"

I told the chaplains what I was experiencing. They all just smiled as if they knew something that I had never thought possible. Scriptures would come alive in my circumstances. I was experiencing the Word and not just reading it! I could see clearly for the first time that God was greater than these steel bars which held me captive! When people would talk to me, I could see things in their character in a compellingly different light. I could see the spirits that were at work in them, whether good or evil. I was no longer looking at people through the eyes of brokenness and the eyes of the flesh, but I could see them through the eyes of Jesus. Everything was amazing!

CHAPTER FOUR

The Encounter

Here I was in the worst possible place on earth, and I had my eyes opened to a realm that I had never known existed. It was a cross between supernatural and freaky to the point that I thought I had finally gone around the bend. I began to write short stories about the visions I was having and record the way the Lord was speaking to me through His Word. I wrote a piece called "The Truth" in which I pitted man's relationship to the world against God's intentions for man. Everyone from the guards to the chaplain's office wanted to read this work.

I was awakened to a visibly stark contrast about who God really was and who the world portrays Him to be. The enemy, Satan, wants us to see ourselves as broken and hopeless. This keeps us vulnerable to his schemes that are meant to keep us from freedom in Christ. But God wants to liberate us from the bondage of sin and all forms of oppression. God's overcoming Spirit turns everything the enemy intended upside down and sets us on a solid foundation.

When I gained this awareness, the attacks of the enemy became worse. I believe that he did not like it at all that I had been set free. During this time, I had been served with divorce papers. The guards were coming by my cell to make sure that I wouldn't try to commit suicide. Little did they know that I had gotten saved and was excited about my life – no matter what the circumstances.

In the ninth month of my sentence, I had finally been taken to the work release block where an inmate can work outside the prison and come back to the prison at night until his time is served. Even though I had a job outside prison, I was not permitted to work outside the prison because I had only been back in Pennsylvania for several months before turning myself in. I was very disappointed that I was not able to work. The child support I owed continued to accumulate.

I was working in the warden's office as a trustee and was a model prisoner for some time. One day when I came back from work my cell had been tossed by the guards. They had found chewing tobacco in the cell. My cell mate worked at Manheim Auto Auction and snuck some chewing tobacco back into the prison one night. When one person brings something into the cell, both inmates are held accountable for the offense.

We were handcuffed, shackled, and shuffled down to this place under the prison which I refer to as the dungeon. Upon arriving, we were confronted by a host of prisoners yelling and screaming as if we had just entered the gates of hell: murderers, rapists, bank robbers and all kinds of grave offenders. We had to sit in there with handcuffs and shackles on at all times. The demonic oppression in that place was so strong that I could feel it. Even the guards seemed like they were part of the dance of pain; they just wanted anyone to step out of line so they could come in and teach them a lesson. That was it! There was no justice in the world and now I was being thrown in hell with the worst of the worst! How could my life get any worse? Where was God? Why was this happening to me after I had given my life to Christ?

Once again, my life began to flash before my eyes. I was overwhelmed with grief and sorrow to the point that I just fell to my knees in brokenness. This was the harsh reality of what my life had come to. I was supposed to be in the hole for a month. My soul was in anguish, vexed, and tormented. I began to weep and cry out to the Lord: "If you are there and really love me like your Word says that you do, then give me a sign and show me that you are with me!" I would have sooner died than to go on like that for another day. I yearned for death to come as all hope seemed to slip away.

In that moment, God showed up! All of the sudden, I saw in my Spirit an illuminated cross. It stretched from heaven to earth. I could see up through it because it rested upon me in my cell. An overwhelming peace permeated the atmosphere! What was happening? How was it possible that God would show up in this dungeon and hear my cry?

The next thing I knew, I started singing songs to the Lord that I didn't even know. All of the demonic activity in the hole went silent as I sang. Even the guards came to see what was going on. While they were asking me if I was alright, I just kept on singing! I had never in my life experienced anything like it.

Who was this God who had the power to cut through steel bars and silence the demonic forces of evil in the very place where they dwell? How was it that He revealed Himself to me in such a profound way in the depths of such a hellish atmosphere? What did this mean? The entire atmosphere had changed in a moment and there was no denying that the presence of the Lord was right there in our midst!

Jesus somehow became a part of me that day. It was much more than an experience; it was a divine encounter. The guards thought that I had a nervous breakdown or that I had lost my mind. When they came back to check on me, I sat there with a peace over me that surpassed human understanding. The other inmates in the hole began to call me "Preach" and would ask me questions about what had happened.

There were Muslims and self-acclaimed atheists down there. They wanted to know about this presence because they knew the atmosphere had changed. I began telling everyone about Jesus, how He had showed Himself to me on that cross, and how He loved them. I told them Jesus was real, a force that no one or nothing, not even the prison bars or concrete walls, could stop. I encouraged them to give their lives to Him. The guards found my story rather fascinating yet remained cynical. Nevertheless, I have carried this experience with me. It has become a part of who I am, indelibly imprinted into me as a mark that I have seen His glory!

After a few days I could be found reading my Bible, singing to the Lord and preaching the gospel to everyone who had ears to hear down in that hole. Bud Roda came down to visit me along with Al Huber, and they heard me singing. The story spread all through the prison. The last two months I was at Lancaster County Prison, I tried to convert the whole block. Even the chaplains said that they were sorry to see me leave.

As I prepared to leave, Bud Roda asked me if I wanted to go to a place called "The Potter's House" to continue the work I had started while in prison. About two weeks before my release I was sitting in my cell praying in the Spirit and the Lord gave me a vision that He was going to build a center for healing in the lives of the broken and addicted on the property that my dad owned along the Conestoga River in Brownstown, Pennsylvania. It was very detailed. I even drew some pictures of it before I left the prison, then wrote it off as a nice but impossible idea.

When I got out of prison, I did go to The Potter's House. My dear friend Bud picked me up on a cold wintry morning in March of 2005 and dropped me off there. I was thrilled to be released but there were many challenges ahead. The reality of responsibilities mounted up on me fast. I went back to the place I worked before going to prison. I had to get up at 4:30 a.m. to catch a 5:00 bus into Lancaster, then catch another bus to Mt. Joy. In the afternoon I would leave Mt. Joy at 4:30 p.m. to catch the bus back to Lancaster and then another bus to The Potter's House in Leola. This amounted to 14-hour days to get to and from work. I then attended classes at The Potter's House in the evening. This went on for seven months and began to wear me down.

It seemed like no matter what I did, I could never get caught up financially. My wife had shown me some grace, but I still owed $14,000.00 in back support for the twelve months that I was incarcerated! It seemed impossible to pay child support, fines and costs, supervision fees from probation and parole and rent at The Potter's House and still be able to pay bus fare and live anything that resembled a normal life.

I pray that everyone reading this can see the challenges that are faced by the people who are trying to return to a "normal" lifestyle after they get out of prison, and why so many don't make it and go back. When you add it all up, the numbers and the stresses are averse to one's ability to manage life in a meaningful and productive way. The cycle only traps a person in poverty. My life was on overload. I was feeling trapped in a vicious struggle to make the ends meet and satisfy all the voices crying for my attention.

I had to make some decisions about how I was going to keep navigating all these waters of adversity. I certainly understood that I had put myself there, but I was pushed to make another decision as to how I could make my life work and have a workable budget that didn't sentence me to an impoverished life.

I decided to call my old boss in Virginia Beach and ask if the position was still open. He was very glad to hear from me and asked when I could come back to work. Even though my driver's license was no longer suspended, and I had acquired a beat up old white pickup truck, there was still not enough opportunity to make a go of it in Pennsylvania. My kids were heartbroken once again that I was leaving the area, but I felt I had no choice. In the community where I was living, it was almost impossible to find a job that paid enough to allow me to meet my obligations.

My mother's condition had stabilized. So in September of 2005 I packed up my truck, said my good byes, and was off to Virginia Beach. I missed my kids terribly but I didn't see any other way at the time to make it work. I had a terrible sense of being alone. Issues seemed like mountains that were impossible to climb. It was easy to get discouraged. I tried my best to stay focused, but the truth was that I was dying inside and life as I knew it would never be the same. My wife wasn't coming back and my chance for redemption in our family looked so dismal. I carried that burden with me for years and I suffered so much depression over it.

Since I was no longer running from the law, I could go back home every couple of months to visit. This was hard on me and the kids. They were experiencing some of the same abandonment that I had experienced as a young man as they tried to grow up in a broken world and make sense of a broken family. I never wanted to do that to my children. My heart was broken that there wasn't a thing I could do to change the reality of my circumstances. I often prayed that God would continue to watch over them and guide their lives in the way everlasting by His mighty hand.

Although I was a lot more at peace, it was still not the same. I had let my kids down again. I prayed constantly that we could be together, but the days and months once again rolled by in a never-ending cycle of coming and going. I tried to get as much time as I could with them. I was sad, but grateful that I had them in my life to a degree. Each time we parted I could feel the pain of the separation over and over. I knew I had a responsibility, but also knew I would fall if I went back to Pennsylvania.

For two years I lived as a long-distance dad. My heart was always burdened by the thoughts of how they must be feeling without me being there. I carried a sense of sorrow and peace at the same time as I tried to man up to my responsibilities when underneath I felt all alone in this world. I knew the experiences I had in prison were very real, but they were being choked out by the cares of this world.

I saw the parable of the Sower in Matthew 13 being played out in my life. I didn't know how to prevent this from being my reality even with all the prayers a human being could muster. "That same day Jesus went out of the house and sat by the lake. Such large crowds gathered around Him that He got into a boat and sat in it, while all the people stood there on the shore. Then He told them many things in parables, saying: "A farmer went out to sow his seed. As he was scattering the seed, some fell along the path, and the birds came and ate it up. Some fell on rocky places, where it did not have much soil. It sprang up quickly, because the soil was shallow. But when the sun came up, the plants were scorched and withered because they had no root. Other seed fell among thorns, which grew up and choked the plants. Still other seed fell on good soil, where it produced a crop- a hundred, sixty or thirty times what was sown. Whoever has ears to hear, let them hear." The disciples came to Him and asked, "Why do you speak to the people in parables?" He replied, "Because the knowledge of the secrets of the kingdom of heaven has been given to you, but not to them" (Matthew 13:1-11).

I got it! I was the seed that had been sown in the thorns. The enemy wanted to choke the seed that was sown in me so that I would not bear fruit in His kingdom. What was I to do? How was

I to change this seemingly impossible situation? How was I to do God's will with all the overwhelming cares that sought to choke this burning fire that had been set ablaze within my soul? There just had to be a way that I could make sense of why I had the encounter and the vision in my prison cell. Why would he choose a broken human being like me to reveal Himself to in the form of that cross, full well knowing that I was probably the least likely to succeed in fulfilling this divine vision.

Oh, how I wanted to follow Him. Oh, how I yearned for His presence—the only place I have ever felt safe and secure. It makes no sense to the human mind how God gave a person total peace when the world seemed to be falling apart and life was crashing down. But He was more real than all my circumstances and greater than my broken heart. This magnificent entity that cut through bars of iron and violently tore through the atmosphere with a peace that surpassed all understanding. Surely there was none like Him in all the earth! How could this be? What did this mean?

In my own understanding, I could not see a way to navigate life's challenges. But somehow, God was calling me to trust Him even as things seemed to be falling apart. Where did all this fit in His plan for my life. What did I need to do to get in alignment with His plan? Things were totally different, yet I was still being broken. Although I was experiencing the pain and sorrow of my failures, He was somehow ahead of me preparing the way. He wanted me to walk by faith and not by what I could see.

This all seemed so strange but so wonderfully safe and real. I just had to trust Him along the way even when I couldn't see His plan. Proverbs 3: 5-6 says "Trust the Lord with all your heart and lean not to your own understanding, but in all your ways acknowledge Him and He will direct your paths." In some strange and beautiful way, it was like I had given the Lord my eyes and in return

He had given me His. He wanted to take me on a journey that I didn't have to figure out; my part was to merely trust Him. It was His plan and His story. He was asking me to abandon my story so He could show me the way home to Him.

This may seem difficult to understand. It was a very difficult thing for me to understand too, but it was more real than my reality, and filled me with more hope than all the hopes and dreams I dreamt on my own throughout my entire life. Somehow, I became intermingled with this entity that was never negative and always saw the best in me even when I felt like a train wreck. He kept gently whispering to me "I want you to stop trying to figure Me out and start opening yourself up to experiencing Me and My plans for your life."

This was weird. Not only did I have an encounter in a prison cell but now I was hearing voices. It was not an audible voice but something deep down inside of me that He would speak to. I could hear Him as plain as day. His voice had a distinct sound. It was like truth that reverberated through the depths of my being. I knew He was the one speaking.

Was this how God spoke to Abraham, Moses and all the patriarchs of faith? Was I actually in a position to hear from the Father of all creation? Was He leading me, guiding me, and directing my life?

As time unfolded the pages of my life, I realized that this was exactly what He was doing. Psalm 32:8 says, "I will instruct you and teach you in the way you should go; I will counsel you with my eye upon you." The more I read His Word, the more I could see His loving eye guiding and directing me. This relationship was beyond words. It is difficult to express the nature of the all-encompassing Spirit that was guiding my life. I knew beyond the shadow of a doubt that He had a plan. I was full of a joyful expectation, knowing that I was a part of that plan. It was not until many years later that the Lord began to reveal that plan. I was living in a paradox between two worlds. All I knew was that God wanted me to trust Him. Somehow, He could weave His glory into the most devastating of circumstances.

This was surely the God of David that wanted to slay all the Goliath's in my life. I had to chase Him and posture myself before Him every day as a lifestyle. The enemy is so crafty when a person finds this place of divine refuge. He wants to sow seeds of doubt and fear. I began to experience attacks from the enemy. I got a call that my mother was getting worse, and my father had another mild heart attack. I was again feeling a tug on my heart that I should go home and be with them. I felt that I would have deep regret for the rest of my life if they passed away and I ignored these promptings.

Once again, I told my friend and employer that my parents were in failing health and I felt that God was asking me to return and spend some time with them. He was so open and receptive and never once portrayed selfishness about having me stay because he had invested so much in me. He genuinely cared about family values above financial gain. I respected him immensely as He modeled that for me. It was so refreshing to be in the presence of someone who genuinely cared about me more as a friend than as an asset to his financial future. I will always hold John Hawley, my boss and my brother, in high regard for the principles for which he stood and the example that he set for others.

In a month or two I wrapped up my responsibilities in Virginia Beach and again headed home. This time I did not have any pending legal issues and I was free to work and see my parents and children with no strings attached. That alone was very liberating to me. As I drove home, I thanked the Lord for all the wonderful friendships I had made and the wonderful opportunities I had been given along the way. I had no idea how I was going to forge a living back home but I knew that God had a plan and that I needed to trust Him in the process. The road seemed long. The different chapters of my life played out again and again in my mind. I was beginning a new chapter in my life with some of the same challenges, but with a sense of hope that I had not felt the other times when I was heading home.

In that mixture of emotions, I had to fight back the urge to allow the enemy to make me second guess what God had clearly laid on my heart. I had to push on and face down my fears. I was perplexed, but not fearful as to why I had made this decision. Many questions were running through my mind, but I also had a real feeling of peace and sense of purpose.

When I arrived, I went to visit my mother. She was so overjoyed to see me. But I noticed that she would slip in and out of reality and sometimes talk about things that made no sense. It made me sad to see this bright, vibrant soul of a woman deteriorating mentally. I knew in my heart why I had made the journey home. I would spend hours and hours with her. We would watch some of the old classic movies that I had watched as a child. I told her often how much I loved her. I thanked her for always being there for me and how grateful I was to have her as my mother. She would give me this sheepish grin and then go off on some other tangent about what happened on the television series "Judge Judy." I would just laugh with her and tell her all the stories of my adventures with the Navy Seals and what an awesome group of men they were.

I would also talk to her about Jesus and share the salvation message of how much God loved her. She would always say that she believed in God but that she was a good person and helped a lot of people so she thought that God would consider her good deeds.

She ran a food bank for the community out of her little apartment for many years after retiring from hairdressing. She fed hundreds of families out of her apartment. The work she did was even covered in the Elizabethtown Chronicle. I would share with her that even though we all were trying to be good people, we had all made mistakes that God would refer to as sins. He wanted to cleanse us and restore us and our relationship with Him so much that He sent His own Son in the person of Jesus to atone for our sins on the cross and restore us back into a right relationship. I told her that I wanted her to go to heaven and that Jesus could make that possible if she would accept Him as her Savior.

My mother shared that she had been hurt by her parents and the church as a young woman. When she married my dad, her parents all but disowned her. She never made church part of her life or ours. It was so sad to hear how she carried those wounds her whole life. I believe that the church has come a long way since the time when my mother was growing up. Back then the standards were very rigid for anyone who wanted to be a member. It was very easy to become labeled an outcast if a person didn't fit into a certain mold. Thank God for His grace and thank Jesus for the cross.

She had just turned ninety and I was certain that she had not accepted Christ and received salvation. I had such a heavy burden for my mom's soul and would talk to her more and more about Jesus as we spent time together. She would say that she had so many questions about Him, and how the missing years of His life in the Bible made her wonder if the Bible was true.

I prayed and prayed that she would have a revelation of who Jesus really was or that He would visit her as He did me. As time passed, her mental faculties steadily deteriorated. It was very clear why God had brought me back despite my own personal challenges. I pleaded with the Lord for her salvation and spent deep times of intercession for her. This was my mother, the woman who raised me and never abandoned me, the woman that God used to bring me into the world. As she and my father were at odds with each other my whole life, I felt torn between the expectations that each of them had for me and the reality that they both had lived totally separated from God's intentions and purposes for their lives. How could they be totally blind to the fact that they were in desperate need of a Savior?

My parents were not aware of the realm of God's Spirit. They were very worldly in the way they thought and processed the issues of their lives. This whole generation was slipping by, and the enemy was stealing the plan of salvation from them. I was distraught over what was taking place spiritually. God had opened my eyes and I could see how the enemy could pass this from generation to generation. But how could it be stopped? Could I be used to break this cycle? I had already made a ton of mistakes.

If it were by my works, then I would not have had a chance. But it was by the grace of God, through faith, that I received salvation. They had to know! They had to be told so that they would not be separated from God for eternity! I didn't know how and I didn't know when, but I was trusting the Lord for breakthrough with my mother and father. I claimed the verse in Philippians 4:13 that says, "I can do all things through Christ, who gives me strength." I was determined to bring them to the Lord.

All of us as human beings are governed by the constraints of time. Our human perception of what is possible is limited by logic and reason. But God is eternal! He lives outside the constraints of time. In essence, we are eternal beings. We are not meant to live as meaningless humans in a meaningless dance called life.

We strive and work hard to retire into years of leisure, then die from lack of purpose. This would be a worldly approach to life and not God's eternal plan of salvation. The enemy has blinded generations of people and given the world a forgery of His original plan for salvation. Material things can too easily become a substitute for the eternal things of God.

I spent the last three years of my mother's life taking care of her needs and just being there with her. These are days for which I will always be grateful. I didn't know when I left Virginia Beach why I was going back, but I felt a tug on my heart. I have learned to be sensitive to God's soft and gentle nudge.

My mother passed on to glory at ninety-two years of age. From the great depression to men walking on the moon to the first biracial president to serve our county, she experienced a lot of change in her lifetime. She was a walking, talking history book and I loved to hear her talk share memories. More than all of that I will always carry her love and encouragement deep in my heart and her memory will also live on in her grandchildren who knew her as Grammy Rain, their version of Lorraine. They will always remember her eccentric way of dressing and her heart for helping the hungry. She was indeed a special lady.

God is so gracious and so caring. He loves us with an everlasting love and will pursue us until our last breath. He is relentless in pursuit of His creation and is jealous for us and our affection toward Him. Such was the case of His pursuit of my mothers' heart and how He sent a pastor to minister the salvation message to her in her eleventh hour. She received salvation even beyond the hurts and the disappointments of her youthful years and the rejection she had experienced from both church and family.

CHAPTER FIVE

Righteous Men Fall

It had been two years since my mother passed. I was working in roofing as a sub-contractor in Hanover, Pennsylvania. On this icy winter day, we were working on a two-story home. Normally we would put safety supports at the bottom of the roof. The catch is that someone has to climb up and set them in place before you can start the tear-off procedure. I had a lot of experience, so I volunteered to go up and set the supports.

The shingles were old and brittle, so I was moving with caution. As I got toward the bottom edge of the roof. I felt the gravel under my feet begin to move. The shingles were icy. As I tried to catch myself, I started to slide! My life began to flash before my eyes. I hit the bottom edge of the roof with my back and all I could feel was an adrenalin rush knowing that I was free-falling from the second story of this house! I knew this was going to be painful! I braced myself for the jolt of hitting the ground, but realized that the first impact was my momentary porch-roof landing. I continued to roll off that roof and, in the blink of an eye, I felt the second jolt of hitting a concrete sidewalk!

At first, I was afraid to check to see if anything was broken. I slowly began to scan my body with my left arm and survey the damage. I noticed that I was bleeding on my side and my knee where I had initially hit the porch roof. I thought that I would be alright until I tried to sit up. A paralyzing pain shot down my leg and across the base of my spine and seized the muscles in my back. The sudden reality of my worst nightmare of ending up paralyzed came over me. That would be the end of my career. I had children to support. How on earth could this have happened to me?

One of the crew members called an ambulance and they came and took me to the emergency room. X-rays revealed that I had blown out the cushions between two of my vertebrae. The pain was from the bone hitting my sciatic nerve and the cushion was gone between the discs that buffers that area from the nerve endings. The only good part was that I hadn't crushed any discs. My roofing career was over! How would I fulfill my obligations? I was so overwhelmed with worry. For the next year and a half, I was unable to work and had to take painkillers to deal with the pain.

Some mornings it was impossible for me to stand up. The pain would shoot down my leg and take my breath away. I would have to slide onto the floor and then pull myself up into a position that would take the pressure off that area of my spine in order to move around to get a painkiller in me before I could function. This was a very dark time in my life. I thought that I may end up crippled and in a wheelchair. I got hooked on the painkillers and would go through severe withdrawal if I didn't have them.

After about a year the painkillers stopped working and I took them just to feel normal. Once again, I was asking God where He had gone and how He could leave me this way. I had to file for disability benefits. I felt totally useless.

For a season, I had a few acquaintances from whom I would get heroin to take away the pain as my tolerance to pain killers was off the charts. I had never done heroin in my life and it's something I swore I would never get into; however here I was all busted up with an opiate addiction and scared to death I would never be normal again. I tried to be a decent dad to my kids, but I would miss some of their sporting events because of being sick from withdrawal. I was becoming everything that I had despised in life. I was trapped in addiction once again after years of being free.

I asked my doctor if there was anything that could be done to help repair my spine because I didn't want to live the rest of my life hooked on painkillers. I prayed that God would please help me find a way out of this life that I had sunk into and heal and restore me. Where did my hunger for Him go? How could I get back to being the man I had become after He came to me in that prison cell? I was desperate and I hated the fact that I was back in an active addiction after having been delivered and free from that life for quite some time.

My doctor referred me to a spinal injury specialist who had done work with others with my exact same injury, and had been effective in most cases. I would avoid surgery with this procedure. After a year and a half of terrible pain, I was open to anything. This was the first time since the accident that I felt a glimmer of hope.

In this procedure, the doctor inverts you on a table and decompress your vertebrae in your discs. When they are decompressed, the doctor injects a silicone substitute and rebuilds the smashed cushions between the vertebrae. I was intimidated by the thought of someone going into my spine with a needle and injecting something into my back near those painful points of pressure. But I was desperate, so I agreed to go along with the doctor's recommendation. The procedure was done several weeks later.

There was a little soreness at the injection site for several days, but "Hallelujah!" I began to be free from pain in a very short time. Within six months I decided to return to roofing. It took some time for me to get back into the swing of things. The procedure was a success, but I did not plan how to get out of the opiate addiction. Before I would go totally down a bad road, I decided to get help.

I will remember the night I decided I was going to get off the pills as long as I live. I was praying with all my heart to God. "Please do not let me continue to go on this way. Deliver me out of the grip these pills have on me." I didn't want to die and leave my children with the legacy of a father who lost his life to a drug addiction. I called around to see what treatment centers may have a place for me and I came across one toward Philadelphia called Eagleville. They found a bed for me the very next day. However, I had no way to get there. I prayed for God's intervention.

I tracked the Greyhound bus schedule and there were no buses that ran close enough to that location. I called everyone I knew to get a ride close to Philadelphia and drop me off at the facility, but for one reason or another no one was available. I was desperate and determined to get there. I remembered how I had pleaded with God for healing for my back and He had been faithful. I remembered my prayers that God would not let me die in an addiction and leave that legacy for my children to remember me by. He was faithful and I was going to keep my promise to Him. He had healed me from the pain, and I was determined to get free from the addiction to the opiates.

My last resort was to catch an Amtrack train to Coatesville, Pennsylvania then get a bus from there to Eagleville. I reasoned with myself that I could just wait for a couple of days and be able to find a ride. But I knew that in a couple of days I would probably change my mind. So at about 7:30 pm on September 6, 2011, I hopped on a train heading for a rehabilitation center in a place that I had never even thought of going.

As I sat and waited for the train, I called my oldest son Jacob who had just started his freshman year at Liberty University. My son said that he was proud of me. He began to sob, saying that he had seen my struggle and wanted me to be healed. He felt that the

Lord was answering prayers we both had prayed. Somehow, God was saying to me through Jacob that He was pleased with me and that it was His time to deliver me. It was the strangest, most surreal way that I had ever heard God's voice, but I knew that it was Him.

A very powerful dynamic takes place in the realm of the Spirit when fathers and sons agree in prayer according to Gods' good and pleasing purpose. It was time for his dad to get healed and the whole family to get healed as well. Somehow, I knew while getting on that train that my life would never be the same and I would never look back. Something happens to people who look back; the ending is not good. When the angel of God rescued Lot's wife out of Sodom as judgment was falling on the city, she looked back. This was against God's command. I believe that she yearned for the life she had in Sodom. When she looked back, she immediately turned into a pillar of salt.

God paid such a dear price to redeem us from the old life and knows that the turning back automatically produces hardness of heart. I believe that this is as true today as it was in the time of Lot. The consequences for turning back never change because God established it to be that way. We must keep our eyes on Jesus and press on to obtain the prize of the high calling He has for us.

Alas, I hopped on the train and about an hour later stepped off at the Coatesville, Pennsylvania station. I was scheduled to catch the last bus out of Coatesville to Norristown and the center said they would pick me up at the bus station there. I sat and waited for the bus to Norristown. After about ten minutes I saw a bus pull up ending their route. I went and asked the driver if he knew when the bus for Norristown would arrive. He told me that I had missed the last bus by about thirty minutes, and would have to wait until morning. It was about thirteen miles to Norristown, but I had no way of getting there! I became very agitated and began to question myself. I thought about taking a train back to Elizabethtown, but quickly came to my senses and realized that this was a test to see if I was serious about getting well. I couldn't get God off my mind. He was working all things out to bring me through this. Somehow, I knew that He had His hand on my life.

I decided that I would walk to Norristown. All through the night I walked up highways and roads that I had never been on before. The journey seemed unending as I began to go through withdrawal from the opiates and my legs were cramping up. I reached the point where I began to scream at God! Was this my punishment for not staying on track with the Lord, I wondered. The miles were daunting. My feet and legs were aching. Finally, around sunrise, I walked exhausted into the town of Norristown.

I called the center and they sent someone to pick me up. When the gentleman arrived, I was so relieved. When I told him how I had gotten there, he told me that with that type of determination he had no doubt I would make it. Upon arrival, they checked my backpack and gave me a physical before taking me into the detox at the hospital. My story spread among the counselors, and I became very close to many of them for the three weeks that I was there.

After three weeks at the center, I was informed that my insurance would no longer pay for my stay. I was worried, but immediately I went into prayer and asked the Lord to direct my steps so that I would not fall. In about two hours I was called to go see a counselor. She told me that they had a recovery house called Stepping Stones in Pottstown, Pennsylvania where I could go. I told them I would pray about it and give an answer the next day. I went back to my room and contended with God. "Pottstown? I have never in my life been in Pottstown, Pennsylvania. Why in the world would I go there?"

On the other hand, if I went back home I knew that I would not fare well. After praying most of the night, I went to sleep and I woke up with a new sense of hope that somehow God was in this, and I needed to trust Him. God would show up in my life again and show me great and mighty things that I did not know. I committed to going to the recovery house that next morning. Three days later I packed my clothes and hopped in a van with the same driver who had picked me up to take me to the center. He dropped me off at the recovery house in Pottstown.

From the moment I arrived at the door, I hit it off well with the house manager who worked in the renovation department. I was able to work with him from the start, earn some money to pay for my stay, and continue to pay child support. After a couple of weeks, he introduced me to the owners of the recovery house, and we struck up a relationship. Before long, I was asked to work for them. They would give me an apartment and a truck to drive so that I could start my own business in Pottstown. These were some very kind and trusting people. They were in real estate and had multiple properties in the area. They hooked me up with a seemingly never-ending supply of renovation jobs. This was precisely my line of work. I was so thankful to have a fresh start in a new place. But there was more going on than the eyes could see. God had a great plan that He was about to reveal.

I marveled that I had gone from a treatment center to a recovery house and in a couple of months was running my own business again, healed, clean and restored. God had brought me full circle in that short time even though for most people it would have taken years! He was there, watching over me and guiding me every step of the way.

God was moving in my life at an accelerated rate. I faced the stark reality that I was not the one who arranged the circumstances. I was being guided by divine oversight. There was no logical explanation that the human mind could comprehend. I started to experience God in ways I had years before. I would read a scripture one day and I could see it playing out before my very eyes the next. I knew it was the hand of God because there was no other way that it could have happened.

I was experiencing and walking in a realm that was not of this world but was being worked out in this world. The songs I would hear would become themes for the work that God was doing. Each day had unfolding glory attached to it in one way or another. Deep things directly from the heart of God were being revealed to me. This was the most amazing relationship that I ever had, and it was not with human beings, it was with the Creator of all things. Somehow, I was connected to His plan and purposes. This is so hard to put into words; I am asking God to write this story and not to let my own logic or reason limit the truth that He wants to reveal in these pages.

I found a church, Zion UCC, that was the oldest church in Pottstown. I felt I was guided there for some strange and wonderful reason. I could almost sense God smiling over me and preparing me for something that I had never imagined. Soon after arriving in Pottstown, I went to the post office to get a change of address form. The post office did not have the forms, so the postmaster directed me to get the form in the neighboring town, Stowe. It seemed very bizarre to me how a post office could run out of change of address forms, but I took it with a grain of salt and set out for the next town.

I had never in my life been in Pottstown, Pennsylvania. Mere circumstances had taken me there. What strange and wonderfully mysterious force had guided me down this path? I felt so close to God in this place, as if I had come home—yet I had never been there before in my life. I would never have chosen to live there if the decision had been in my hands.

All my life I had struggled to find my place and my identity despite all the brokenness and dysfunction I had experienced growing up. I had tried to build my life out of a broken past and a broken family with a broken lens. I never seemed to be able to create a meaningful and purposeful life that lasted more than a few years. Then circumstances and situations would come and alter the course of my life. Now, there was a sense of safety and permanence. I felt safe in the hands of something or someone that was much greater than I. In my heart I knew it was God, but if I were to tell people what I was experiencing, they would have probably thought I was delusional.

I felt the hand of God on my life more profoundly than I had ever experienced since doing time in Lancaster County Prison. I trusted that He held me in the palm of His hands. I had this nervous excitement that I could not shake. I asked God to show me what He was doing and what He was trying to teach me. In my spirit I felt that a major revelation or breakthrough was on the way and that the secrets of His plan would soon be revealed.

God is intimately involved in every detail of our lives but often we are not in tune or in step with how He is speaking. Jeremiah 29:11-13 says, "For I know the plans I have for you, declares the Lord, plans to prosper you and not to harm you, plans to give you hope and a future. Then you will call on me and come and pray to me, and I will listen to you. You will seek me and find me when you seek for Me with all your heart." Here I was, living in these very words as if they were guiding me and protecting me. Somehow, they were living inside of me, and I was walking them out. God was leading me to a destination that had not yet been revealed.

In Romans 8:29-30 the Word says, "For those God foreknew, He also predestined to be conformed to the image of His Son, that He might be the firstborn of many brothers and sisters. And those He predestined, He also called, those He called, He also justified, those He justified, He also glorified." These words resonated with me to my core. Many people go through life and discount things that happen as mere circumstances, yet so much takes place in the spiritual realm.

CHAPTER SIX

The Inheritance

This was the point at which God began to reveal Himself to me in ways that I could never have imagined. No other answer apart from a revelation of God's plan could be sufficient to explain the series of events that began to unfold. This is a story of the divine orchestrations of God.

As I mentioned in the previous chapter, I had to go to another town to get a change of address form when moving into my apartment in Pottstown. I decided to walk to Stowe because it was a beautiful, sunny day. As I walked under an old iron bridge on Route 100 in Pottstown, I looked to the right and saw a huge estate. A plaque in the front indicated that it was a historical site. The lawn was well manicured and the grounds looked as if they played an important part in history. As I moved closer to the house and plaque, an intense feeling came over me that I had been there before. I even thought for a moment that I detected the faint smell of my mother. It was a type of altered reality. I felt for a moment I was trapped in time and God had stopped me right there. There was such a profound sense of home at that place. I did not want to leave the moment, but I had other things to accomplish that day.

The closer I got, the stronger the feelings became. My heart was beating as if there were a climactic event unfolding. As I came to rest in the very front of the property and beheld the full view of the estate, I looked down at the sign that read: "Pottsgrove Manor, the home of John Potts founder of the town of Pottstown, Pennsylvania. Founded in 1752 and formerly known as Pottsgrove."

It felt like reality had shifted in the core of my soul. You see, my mother's maiden name was Potts and she had died the year before I came to Pottstown. It was like God was showing me a deep, rich heritage that had been lost for most of my life. It seemed that He had navigated my life's journey to lead me to this moment. I can't even put into words what I experienced that day. My life changed when I happened upon that sign.

God put it on my heart to do an in-depth search into the lives of the Potts family. I wanted to link the pieces of the puzzle together. I began to spend my time at the library and the historical society to gain deeper insight into the life and the character of this family. I found out that the church I had been attending, referred to as the "Old Brick Church," was built on land donated to Pottstown by John Potts for the purpose of religious practices.

I discovered that Thomas Potts, father of John Potts, had come directly from England in the late 1600's and had landed at the port of Philadelphia on the invitation of William Penn. He was fleeing religious persecution under the rule of King Charles II. These people were Quakers by faith and would not take up arms since it was against their beliefs. They had to escape from England or suffer the loss of land and title as well as be thrown into prison. You see, back then if you did not go to war for king and country, your property would be confiscated, and you would be imprisoned. In 1732 Thomas Potts settled in Germantown, Pennsylvania, and had a few sons, one of whom was John. John Potts migrated east and founded the town of Pottstown in 1752.

The family was known for iron mastery in England and the craft came with them as well as with the Rutters and Nutt families. They purchased 100,000 acres of land for the purpose of iron mastery from William Penn, the founder of Pennsylvania. John Potts had eight sons who founded all of the iron furnaces in several counties. "Penn's Woods" was the name for Pennsylvania when William Penn arrived in this country. King Charles II owed a debt of $89,000 to the father of William Penn as he was a shipping merchant and an Admiral in the Royal Navy in England. When Penn's father died, the king gave William Penn one million acres of land in the new world as payment of the debt. I doubt that King Charles II realized what he had done.

Within six months, I became quite the historian regarding the founding fathers of Pennsylvania and of our country. Out of the Potts family came the Hopewell, Warwick, Joanna, Cornwall Furnaces as well as the Martic Forge. It was through the Martic Forge in Lancaster County that I had made the connection between the Potts families in Pottstown, Montgomery County and Lancaster County and my lineage.

It was fascinating to learn who these people were and understand the part they played in the industrial revolution of our country. They forged the first Ben Franklin stove which kept many settlers warm through cold Pennsylvania winters. I did not confirm this through any authentic documentation, but my own personal findings and the circumstances surrounding my discovery were proof enough for me to believe that God had led me here to validate a spiritual heritage that I would never have found otherwise.

I later found out that George Washington used Pottsgrove Manor as a strategic headquarters in the Battle of Valley Forge and that he was a close personal friends of John and Ruth Potts. George and Martha Washington had frequented Pottsgrove Manor and slept there often. He referred to John as "Dear Mr. Potts" as I found in an article which indicated that George Washington had an affection for them as close personal friends. This was an amazing walk through the pages of history and my heritage from my forefathers. I also found a letter in the public archives of one Benjamin Franklin endorsing Jonathan Potts (son of John Potts) to attend Oxford University in England to become a doctor.

I mean—really? These are the stories I grew up with in history class in school. And they were within my family line! This amazing family tended to the wounded in the Battle of Valley Forge in service to our nation as it was being won from British tyranny. This led to winning independence in 1776. The Potts family had the first contract with George Washington to forge the cannons at Hopewell Furnace for the Revolutionary War. It was not the service that they did for our country but their deep faith that fascinated me. What they believed became more important to me than what they did for a living.

The Potts family had followed God across the ocean to a New World with no foreknowledge of where they were going. As men and women of deep faith, they believed in God and in the sanctity of freedom and human life. For the next year or two I relished this newly awakened part of my heart. Roots of faith were deeply planted in my background, yet it took nearly fifty years of my life for God to reveal this to me. I received my inheritance during that time, and it was not an inheritance of gold or silver. It was of much more value. Hope and dignity were given to me directly from the hand of my Creator. A character of integrity girded me with a spiritual heritage that all the riches in the world cannot buy. Somehow God had used this to set me on a course to fulfill a destiny that I would have never been able to think of or create in my own thoughts or plans. Surely this was the hand of God and He had been guiding me all my life. Now I could see it!

This was not a natural inheritance whereby a parent wrote a will which led to transfer of land or wealth. It was a spiritual inheritance given to me from above that spanned hundreds of years. I deeply understood that this was what had been missing all my life. God bestowed me with my identity, my purpose, and a sense of direction for my life. I will be forever grateful for this discovery and how it totally changed the essence of how I looked at myself, the world, and my place in it.

I read books on the Quakers. They were known as "The Quiet People" and also "The Friends." Their Christian roots could be traced to the early 1700's in England. They became part of the Anabaptist movement in the formative years of our country. It was from that perspective that God began to shape and mold my character. My life was anything but a "Quiet People" experience, but I had inherited the same sense of peace as that of my heritage. On a light note, I could say that I became a little more like John the Baptist in my relationship with God and the shaping of my spiritual identity.

A boldness emerged in my witness and my approach to life. My time working with the U.S. Navy Seals seemed to be part of my preparation and my training, giving me laser-sharp focus in whatever I set out to do. I started a ministry of texting scriptures to certain people every morning. It began with ten or so people and as of today it has grown to over three hundred. I refuse to start my day without spending a minimum of an hour with God and in the Word. I believe that this discipline came from my time in Virginia Beach under the leadership of the retired Navy Seals. I had transferred this to a spiritual approach and to my relationship with God.

I chase God! I wake up every morning and look for Him in everything. I wake up and wait for the sunrise so I can hear the birds start to chirp and watch the beautiful display of the Lord's symphony of life from the rising of the sun to the setting of the sun. I ponder the vast magnitude of things that He commands every day from the migration of the animals to the changing of the seasons, to the twinkling of the stars in the sky to the roar of the ocean waves.

He keeps it in motion; spring, summer, fall and winter continue in perfect harmony in a never-ending cycle since the dawn of creation. His love has never failed mankind. Although mankind fails perpetually, He still chooses to love us.

This is such a marvelous mystery. Exodus 20:6 says, "But I lavish My unfailing love for a thousand generations on those who love Me and obey My commands." What a wonderful promise from the mouth of God to the generations of men. Oh, that I would have been brought up to know Him! But there was still time left to fall in love with my Father in heaven. I was not going to waste another day searching for life outside of that relationship. He had revealed His heart toward me and like a magnet, I could not resist His love. I have not turned aside from that pursuit since the day He met me in front of that estate in Pottstown, Pennsylvania.

It dawned on me that, when I was a child, my mother took us out to French Creek which is a part of the original Hopewell Furnace in Montgomery County. Why would she have taken me there? Did she know that she had a heritage there yet never shared it because of the hurt she received through her parents? Or maybe she thought I was too young to understand. I will only know the answers when I get to heaven.

I would get up early on Saturday mornings and drive out to French Creek to watch the sunrise on Hopewell Lake. It became a holy place for me. I would sense God in this setting in the early hours of the morning in ways that can not be humanly described. I was being cradled in His loving arms as we would sit together and watch creation come to life. I felt the warmth of His loving smile upon my heart as I was filled with delight at the reality of His presence.

Words cannot describe the experience of "a raptured heart," but these are the only words I can use to describe the love affair that I was having with God. He was so holy and so beautiful; all I could do was hunger and thirst for more of Him. In Psalms 42:1-2 the sons of Korah wrote, "As the deer pants for the water, so my soul pants for you, my God. My soul thirsts for God, for the living God. When can I go and meet with God?" Indeed, I shared with the Psalmist that passionate hunger for God's presence in my life. I was lost without Him. He was the meaning behind everything that I was becoming.

One beautiful sunny day in the summer of 2011 I decided to go for a walk along the bank of the Schuylkill River. The river ran through the town of Pottstown and separated it from the town of Coventry. There was a dock in a park directly across the bridge from Pottstown. It looked like an awesome place. I packed up some snacks and some research notes on the Potts family and went to sit at the dock.

From the dock, I had a panoramic view of the entire town of Pottstown. As I was praying in the Spirit, I began to see in the spirit the founding and the evolution of the town whose heritage I now knew and claimed as mine. It was surreal. I could see building after building being erected and torn down and the sounds of horse hooves clacking on the roads as if I were in a different time in history. Then it would come undone like a fast-moving time lapse photography being played out in my mind with the history of the town unfolding in my heart. I knew that God wanted to show me the evolution of this town in history for some strange and wonderful reason. As I sat, I began to have a vision from God that brought rebuilding the city into mind. I would use that vision to draw a card for the business of "Pottstown Remodeling" with a cross in the very center of the picture.

The cross of Christ was the center of everything. I seemed to be swept back to the vision I had in my prison cell so many years ago as if God were telling me that this would be the center upon which my life would be built. As I was staring at this picture of this cross, I looked up and saw two doves flying through the air. The doves had scriptures on their wings. The first scripture was Psalm 127:1 "Unless the Lord builds the house, the builders labor in vain. Unless the Lord watches over the city, the guards stand watch in vain." I placed the notation of Psalm 127:1 in the top right-hand corner of the card.

The second scripture was from Genesis 14:20: "Then Abraham gave Melchizedek a tenth of everything." Who was Melchizedek? His name means "king of righteousness," a prototype of Jesus. He also was known as priest of the Most High with no genealogy from which He could be traced; this is also true of Jesus as He was born by the power of the Holy Spirit. I placed this scripture reference in the top left-hand corner of the card. God was speaking to me on the importance of giving a tenth of all my earnings to His church for the work of His kingdom.

In a short time, two more doves appeared. They also were carrying scriptures on their wings. The first was Isaiah 51:1-2: "Listen to me, you who pursue righteousness, you who seek the Lord: look to the rock from which you were hewn, and to the quarry from which you were dug. Look to Abraham your father and Sarah who bore you; for he was but one man when I called Him, that I might bless him and multiply him." I placed this in the bottom left-hand corner of the card. It was as if God was giving me a framework for something that He had planned for me to do. What was He saying to me and why was He showing me these things? What was He preparing me for?

The final scripture was Romans 8:28: "And we know that all things work together for good to those who love the Lord, to those who are called according to His purpose." This sealed all the other scriptures together as if it was a covenant that was being established by God for a work that I was supposed to do. The vision was more real to me than any human experiences or interactions I have ever experienced. I put this in the bottom right-hand corner of the card. I saw it as a final word on the blessing of the work that He had for me to do. When the vision passed, part of me just seemed to fall into the card as if my spirit was being poured into it. I fell into a spiritual realm that was so very real.

The Lord told me to look at the water of the Schuylkill River. As I did, I felt as if I were being poured into the river. I looked down the river and I saw it dump into the ocean and then I saw the ocean become a shore. I realized that I was being transported in my spirit to the shores of England from where my forefathers had come. I saw the journey that they had taken to America. I saw the wars in Europe and the battles that were fought for king and country and the exodus of my ancestors. I was then swept away further into the holy lands. I saw many different kingdoms rise and fall. I saw the building and the destruction of the Tower of Babel. I witnessed the dispersion of the people from that place and the migration of my family to Europe. Then there were holy wars and I saw the taking of Jerusalem by King David and the captivity under Zedekiah to Nebuchadnezzar in Babylon. I saw the temple being rebuilt at the time of Nehemiah as events flashed before my eyes one after the other. It was as if I was there.

I saw the crucifixion and the price that was paid for the whole world to be redeemed on that cross. Then, in a moment's time, I came back to my senses. Whoa! What had just happened to me? I thought I was beginning to lose touch with reality. I began to sob and pray: "God, if this was really from You and not a self-conjured vision, then give me a sign that it was real. Please show me that You are the One who transported me through time and space with You in my spirit. Confirm that I really saw all of these things. Please, God. Please make it known to me that this was you!"

As I tried to collect myself, a boat came toward me. The middle-aged man who was driving the boat began to pull up to the dock. When he saw me, he yelled, "Hello, can you tie off this rope to the dock for me?" I gladly obliged and grabbed the rope as he tossed it to me. As he stepped off the boat, he saw that I had my Bible laid out on the dock. He noticed that I was drawing a picture with scripture references written on the paper.

He asked if I was an artist. I explained that I was doing some research on my family tree and found this to be a good place to sit and think. He then asked what family tree I was researching since he had a lot of knowledge about the history of the area. I told him that it was the Potts family because they were a part of my heritage. He reached out to shake my hand and said with a smile, "I need to tell you something. My name is Robert Potts!"

What were the odds of him pulling up on a boat at this dock, at this moment, and finding one of his distant relatives sitting there studying the Potts family heritage? This was the affirmation that I needed to convince me that this vision was definitely from God.

We were both amazed. It was only providence that caused us to meet. As he loaded his boat on his trailer and we said our good-byes, I realized that I had just received my confirmation from God. I left there and called my oldest son Jacob to tell him what had happened. He knew that I had been having encounters with God and he was ecstatic about what was happening. It was clear to all my sons that I had found my God and in doing so I had found myself.

During this time my sons had been coming to visit me during the weekends and we would often go on tours through Pottsgrove Manor.

I would tell them the story of how God had shown Himself to me and what that meant for them as well. They loved the times when they could come because it was equally rewarding for them to learn about this history that was their heritage, too. We came together as father and sons during that time, bonding in a precious way. I thanked God so much for bringing each one of us to this place where things started to make sense and we began to come into our own as a family again. Those days were vividly supernatural as God was showing me great and mighty things which I did not know!

Come summer, I became the caretaker of the Potts burial grounds that were located behind the "Old Brick Church." It was quite an experience to walk over my fifth, sixth, and seventh-generation ancestors' graves. I took delight in caring for it since it was also a historical site and was gated with a stone wall around it. I was baptized in the church and became a member. I was privileged to meet the mayor of Pottstown and tell her the story behind the story. She was fascinated by how God had brought me to this town. Although I had felt as if I had come home and found my spot in the world, God still was not done with me. He had yet to unfold the purpose for which I had been shown all these things.

I stayed in Pottstown for over two years. In 2012 I got a call from my sister telling me that my dad was very sick. She asked me to go visit him. My relationship with my father was very rocky. Part of me did not want anything to do with going back there; the other part of me did not want him to die without us reconciling the past and the trauma that affected me so severely. I prayed and prayed about going back. I finally asked God to give me the courage to see my dad and in some way make peace between us. This was very hard for me. I had a ton of ill feelings toward this man. I had lived my life in fear of Him for many years. He had a way of bringing anger out of me and I wanted to let that part of my life die. But this, apparently, was part of God's plan for my redemption.

CHAPTER SEVEN

The Call

I went to see my father in the spring of 2012. As I walked into his little shack along the Conestoga River in Brownstown, Pennsylvania, a myriad of memories came rushing into my head. I wanted to turn around and leave before I would even see him. He had lived on this property for thirty years. It was a junk yard on the outside and a hoarder's dream on the inside. He collected everything. The place had not been cleaned in a long time. His long-time girlfriend Judy lived with him for almost twenty years. She had come down with Crones Disease and her health was failing, so neither one of them were in any shape to take care of the property or house.

The looks of the place reflected the condition of his life and the messed-up feelings that I had about my upbringing. There was an evil spirit of death and sorrow in the atmosphere that weighed so heavily on my soul. Why did I leave my life to come back here and enter this atmosphere of horrible memories and bad feelings? What was the purpose? The last thing I wanted at this point in my life was to experience any more feelings of hatred or degradation coming from this angry old man who I knew as my father. No one had seen me come in, so I thought of just turning around to leave. Nobody would ever know I had been there.

All of the sudden I heard a cough in the background. I knew it was him. He started talking to his dogs who were his constant companions. He sounded like he was in fairly good spirits, so I gathered what infinitesimal fortitude I had and started to walk toward his bedroom. This is where he spent most of his time. As I approached his door, he caught a glimpse of me. He smiled and said that he was really glad I was coming to visit.

Something was wrong! When I laid eyes on him, all the feelings of animosity disappeared and a sense of feeling sorry for him took their place. I couldn't put my finger on what was different, but gradually realized that what was different was me. I was seeing him through the eyes of Jesus instead of the eyes of resentment for the first time! This was so wonderfully bizarre, as he had not changed at all. He still cursed a lot, told dirty jokes and called people names to make himself feel adequate. But I could somehow see past all of that. I could see the brokenness of a man who had been through hell on earth, experienced the trauma of war, and was just responding to life out of those harsh realities.

The impact of my experience in Pottstown altered my entire perception of who I was. I was no longer a broken man who grew up in a broken family, fractured by dysfunction and lack of integrity. I had been adopted into the family of God. I had a new life and a new identity. I could walk with integrity and rise above my feelings and step into my character that Jesus made possible for me to become. This was amazing. I felt like a brand-new man.

It was so freeing to feel acceptance instead of tension between my dad and I. This helped me rise above the past and accept him just as he was. I was not being controlled by toxic emotions or by memories of the past. I was free, and I knew that deep down inside I could stay free. He could no longer own my emotions or make me feel any way I didn't want to feel. Neither him nor anyone else had the right to steal my peace and keep me from walking in the character that I had come to love in myself. I was no longer a man that could be toyed with and forced to engage in the drama of a twisted relationship or dialogue. I had the right to draw healthy boundaries.

There is an authority that we are given over the principalities that seek to bring out the worst in us or in others. This is given to all God's sons and daughters to one degree or another. I could actually see the demonic entities that were at work in people's hearts—not just my dad's but almost everyone I knew. God had given me a great gift and now I could discern between the person and the behavior that they were displaying. I could somehow separate the two and minister to the person without feeding the behavior. It was an empowering that God had given me for a greater work that He intended for me to do. Ephesians 6:12 says, "For our struggle is not against flesh and blood, but against the rulers, against the authorities, against the powers of this dark world and against the spiritual forces of evil in the heavenly places."

My prayer is that people would stop allowing the enemy to cloud and complicate this relationship of love that God wants us all to have with Him. Accept His glorious plan of salvation for your life and receive the adoption and the inheritance which allows you to see things through the lens of the scriptures and not the broken lens of the world. Jesus died to give you an incredible lifestyle that is powerfully positive in every way. He gives us the ability to live an ascended life that is nothing like the thinking and behavior of the world around us. We have been given divine weapons in the spiritual realm to demolish the strongholds of the enemy and take back that territory for the glory of God and the salvation of others.

After my first visit with my father, I left feeling totally at peace. Somehow, through the power of forgiveness and the discovery of my heritage in Him, I was not only able to overcome my own past, but also have the authority to begin taking back ground in the lives of others—including the life of my father whom I had spent a lifetime trying to run away from. This was so delightfully intriguing. I felt that God wanted to use me to change the course of a generation beginning with my own, then embrace the task of helping others find freedom. The same freedom that I had found was the ministry God was calling me into. I sincerely believe that was when I found my calling in life and became empowered to multiply the ministry of reconciliation that He had done in my life into the lives of others.

From that time on, the relationship I had with God changed. I had a deeper sense of passion to work with those who had gone through similar hardships. At first, I would come back down to Lancaster County to visit my dad and share some of my stories with him, but I did not share the encounters that I had with God. He was a cynical and sarcastic kind of guy. Although he would say that it was God who saved his life in Korea, he wanted nothing to do with the church. He spewed animosity toward black people, oriental people, white people, Mennonites, Lutherans, Catholics and every other denomination he could name. He felt that they were all crooked and two-faced. He would tell me that they were out to coerce me into their cults and then rob me blind. I would just listen in dismay. I had encountered a very different God than the one he portrayed through his own brokenness.

As months went by, my father's health continued to decline. My sister kept asking me to go help him. He had frequent VA appointments and his girlfriend was too sick to take him. I was starting to feel pressured by my sister to return to Lancaster, but I did not see how I could.

One weekend my dad asked me to go to the Sharp Shopper in Leola to pick up some groceries. As I was driving there, I passed the Hoover farm where the Potter's House had been that I had gone to some seven years prior. Out of the corner of my eye I saw the owner, Lloyd Hoover and the chaplain from the Lancaster County prison, Al Huber, standing at the end of the lane. Al was the one who led me to the Lord. Like a force from out of nowhere, my steering-wheel turned in that driveway. I hopped out of my truck and started talking to these dear men from my past.

There was a precious anointing in that reunion. After praying together, we exchanged phone numbers. Though I did not expect to see them again, that encounter kept coming back to my mind. I wondered how anything could be a coincidence in God's grand scheme of things. I had been having these amazing encounters with God and it seemed like He was going before me to prepare the way. This was not to be the last time that we would be brought together.

My father was getting worse by the week and was unable to take care of himself much at all. My sister pleaded with me to come back to Lancaster County and take care of my dad, but it was the last thing in the world that I had on my radar to do. I mean, this man had left me when I was a child. I had been traumatized my entire childhood and into my teen years and beyond. Why would I subject myself to any more of this drama when God had given me a new life and a fresh start? I had left a lucrative career in Virginia Beach to come back to Pennsylvania to care for my mother the last years of her life. Why was I the one being elected to take care of this crazy old man? I felt that I did not even owe him an explanation as to why I would not come back to this place of my painful childhood and teenage years.

My sister kept prodding me, telling me that her health was too bad as well and she could not keep going down to look after him. I suggested that he go into a care facility, since he had VA benefits and my Uncle Earl had left him a small fortune as an inheritance. He could afford the care. I felt it was so unfair to put me in that position after all that I had suffered at the hands of this man. Yet, as I kept going to check in on him, the Lord was giving me eyes to see Him as He did, and ears that shut out the degrading remarks and profanities he would often spew out.

Shortly after my encounter with Lloyd Hoover and Al Huber, I received a call from Lloyd asking me if I would come and give a testimony at a men's breakfast they were sponsoring at the Potter's House. This was a weekend that my son Jacob would be coming home from college to visit so I asked Lloyd if Jacob could come along. Lloyd gladly welcomed Jacob and said he wanted us to meet with the local newspaper reporter to do a story on how God had restored my relationship with my son. We were surprised, but we thought it would be an honor to do an article on family restoration.

A week or two before that my dad and sister had looked at a beautiful 32-foot camper with electric bump outs in the living room and bedroom areas. They had asked me if I would like to have it as a place to stay when visiting my dad. I felt this was a form of manipulation. My dad had plenty of money, but a heart of coercion and manipulation. Yet because it was getting expensive to keep paying for hotel rooms when I visited, I told them it would be fine if they got the camper. I had a 2500 Chevy diesel truck for business that could pull the camper to the site in Brownstown. This was now my place to stay when I went to visit my dad. A little while later I was back in Pottstown, and I had a title show up for the camper in my name. Really? I never expected my family to buy this camper for me. I felt many mixed emotions about the gesture and the motive behind the gesture. I was torn between calling them to appreciate their thoughtfulness and reminding them that their tactics would not work.

So many things were going on simultaneously that it was hard to discern what was from God and what was a manipulative move from my family. I prayed and I prayed about how to respond to this gift that had a lot attached to it that I really did not want. My sister assured me that my dad was trying to show me his love; this was the only way he really knew how to express that to me. He was never good at expressing emotions unless they were harsh emotions. I was on my guard. I came before the Lord saying, "Examine my heart Lord, and see if there be any wicked way in me."

I didn't want to have a critical spirit because that is what I despised about my dad. I wanted to give him a chance if his motives were genuine. What if I had become as stubborn and obstinate as I had experienced him to be? Would that make me any better than the man I was trying so hard not to become? What if I was judging him and not allowing him the opportunity to make amends for the past? What if Jesus hadn't forgiven me for all the rotten things that I had done? The questions kept rolling through my mind over and over until I heard the Lord speaking with Matthew 16:15: "But if you do not forgive men their trespasses, your heavenly Father will not forgive your trespasses." I was busted—seared with conviction to the core! I realized I would be such a hypocrite if I didn't forgive him. I would actually be disqualified for the blessings that God wanted to release into my life.

Truly, I have found that forgiveness is the key that unlocks the door to freedom. It was the central theme of the work of the cross and it makes all healing and reconciliation possible.

To forgive is one of the hardest things to do as a human being. Without Christ, bitterness and resentment will keep us trapped for a lifetime. I want to ask you, dear reader, to examine your own heart and see if there is any root of bitterness or unforgiveness that has taken you captive. If you find that you are holding unresolved forgiveness, please go before the Lord and ask Him to set you free from this tool of the enemy. God can release newness of life into your heart and freedom in your mind that you desperately need. The enemy wants to keep you enslaved by resentment until you are poisoned with bitterness.

Bitterness can cause physical health problems. The stress of it can cause heart attacks and strokes. If you knew that something was killing you, would you want to find a cure to keep it from progressing? Forgiveness is God's remedy for the roots of bitterness that come along with deep resentment. Forgiveness can put you on the path to soundness of mind, body and spirit. There is no room for unforgiveness in the heart of someone who is walking with Christ for it can keep us from being fruitful and doing the things that God has called us to do.

After that, my dad and I came to a place where we both felt it was time to let go of the past and try to make the best of the time that we had left. I accepted the camper and started coming back to Lancaster County on the weekends. I will never regret the time we had to spend with each other, no matter how twisted the past was. Both of us had to move beyond it if healing would ever bear fruit in either of our lives.

During this time, I did some volunteer renovations at the Potter's House. I found a recovery club in the area that I would frequent when I was there for the weekends. I also began to attend a church in the area by way of invitation from Lloyd Hoover who was the bishop of the district in which the church was located. It was very convenient since my dad's property was right down the road from the church.

It was physically taxing on me to work all week in Montgomery County and then drive down to Lancaster County every Friday night, stay for the weekend, return and be ready for work on Monday morning. Several times when I had projects in Montgomery County, I would take my camper up to French Creek and park it there for a week or two and then go to my dad's place. I started to get more work in Lancaster County than in Montgomery County and I had to make a decision. Do I stay in Pottstown, or do I save myself a lot of travel and sleep and move to the camper on my dad's property?

The answer became very clear when Lloyd Hoover approached me and asked me if I would consider serving on the Board of Directors for the Potter's House Ministry. I was being called to this area and to the ministry that I had left many years ago. I had learned so much about God and about the redemptive power of the finished work of the cross through the sacrifice of Jesus Christ our Lord and Savior. I had grown so much in God's kingdom and had been given my inheritance from God. This was not the work of any man, and I knew it! This was all my preparation for something that God had been building behind the scenes in the pages of my life.

Somewhere deep down in my heart I could hear God saying, "Finish the work I have started in you."

"What work, Lord?" I asked. "What are you saying?" I had been trained to listen for the voice of the Lord. I knew when he was speaking that it was a very profound reason. All I knew at that point was that He was asking me to trust Him. It was up to me to be obedient to His prompting or decide to follow another path.

I had been at a place many times before where two options in front of me both looked like sound decisions. Then I would hear God say, "This is a choice you will have to make. I will be with you any way you choose to go." I was reminded that free will does indeed have a place in God's plan for our lives. He is a good God who wants us to choose our paths wisely. I stood at a fork in the road. If I stayed in Lancaster, I could see my kids more often and could work on getting the junk yard that my dad lived in cleaned up a bit and do some renovations and repairs on the cabins. I could spend time helping my dad as I did my mother and not leave him alone in the world without anyone to care for Him.

If I remained in Pottstown, I could create a thriving business, do well financially, get involved in recovery and maybe ask to get on the township historical society. The sky was the limit as I was quickly gaining a reputation that was enhanced by the fact that I had deep roots in the community. Even though I had only been there a couple of years, God was accelerating the growth of everything I did and was blessing me abundantly. Was it all about me or was it about the call on my life? This would be the guiding factor in the choice that I was about to make and the beginning of a move of God unlike anything I had ever imagined.

I made the decision to move back to Lancaster County and take care of my dad and serve with Potter's House Minisry. It didn't make a lot of sense, but somehow, I knew it was the right thing. I walked away from my personal ambitions once again to follow this unknown path that God had opened before me. I just had to take a step in faith that God had a plan for my life and that this was part of that plan. Certain aspects of this move were very appealing. I would be helping people who wanted to have a relationship with the Lord and would be serving the recovering community that I had become a part of since coming back to the area.

When moving back, I had deep peace about the decision that I had made. For the next three years I served on the Board at the Potter's House Ministry and volunteered in my spare time. I was very content with the lifestyle that I was living as I spent time with my kids and they could go camping with me just by coming to visit me at my dad's property. I would take days here and there and run my dad to the veterans hospital in Lebanon for his appointments. I enjoyed the freedom of being useful to God and others without massive expectations being put on my shoulders or a ton of drama in my life. Yes, life was good, and I was at peace with God, myself and even my dad. These indeed were truly the simple miracles of life and walking in the spirit with our Lord.

While I was volunteering at The Potter's House, I came up with the idea to have pig roasts on my dad's property. One hundred people showed up to the first one in 2014. The following year, a large crowd of around two hundred people attended. We would have worship music and sweet fellowship down in these woods along the Conestoga River. There was an anointing on this property that couldn't be described. It was as if God was present there and He had earmarked that place for a divine purpose.

During the first year back in Brownstown, there was a change of pastors at the church that I was going to. The new pastor, Samuel Mwangi, happened to be from Kenya, Africa. He had one of the biggest smiles I have ever seen. He was also a full-time drug and alcohol counselor at a local outpatient Christian counseling center. We became good friends and developed a kinship as brothers in a short time. Lloyd Hoover and I had begun to develop a spiritual mentor kind of relationship, him being a spiritual father to me. The director of The Potter's House Ministry at the time was Lanny Millette. He was a soft spoken and very dear man who loved the Lord and wanted to see people saved. We all grew deep in friendship in a couple of years.

CHAPTER EIGHT

It's Time to Love Again

In 2014, the church started a care group that included Lloyd Hoover and his wife Elaine, Pastor Samuel and his wife Gladys, Lanny and his wife Debbie, and—me. Yes, they invited that guy who lived in a camper in the woods like John the Baptist and who had been a loner for over a decade. I was honored to be in the team, but always felt like the odd man out. They didn't intend to make me feel like I didn't belong, but I had come to Jesus through a very different path than the traditional church family route. It's amazing how the same Jesus who saved them is the same Jesus that saved me! Each of us had been shaped and molded by the environment we were born into.

Some people are raised in dysfunctional, broken environments and others in a family with strong Christian values. Jesus is Lord of us all and we all come to salvation through the same Lord. Ephesians 2:14-15 states, "For He himself is our peace, who made both groups one and tore down the dividing wall of hostility by abolishing the law of commandments expressed in ordinances, that He might create in Himself one new man in place of the two, thus making peace." What a beautiful promise that salvation is all inclusive. Jesus died that all could come to salvation! Yes, all, meaning the whole world, not just those who are religious in nature or lifestyle.

I felt so loved and accepted by these men and women of God in my core group. I sensed a feeling of belonging in God's family. I did not have to put on a fake face when I was around them. They accepted me just as I was, broken and in a beautiful process in my walk with the Lord. I didn't have to have it all together to be part of the crowd and I didn't have to compare myself to anyone. Jesus was our common denominator.

I went for a couple months to this care group. One night an adorable little lady showed up. She was an old friend of Lloyd's. Her name was Beth. She shared a bit of her journey with us that night and it sounded like she had been through a lot of the same relational devastation that I had. She also spoke about having attended the Lancaster School of the Prophetic. I had attended that school as well and thought it a bit peculiar that neither of us remembered having seen the other there. However, I wrote it off as coincidence and assumed she was going to be just another member of our care group.

As time went on, we would greet each other at church—but not more than that. One night I received an email sent to the group for prayer for Beth's daughter Tecia and her struggle with a rare form of arthritis. I replied that I would gladly keep her in my prayers. She thanked me for my sentiments, and we started to email back and forth.

One night when I was making spaghetti sauce, I asked through email if she and her daughter would want some of my "famous spaghetti" for dinner. We had just been in contact through a group email. I knew that she had never seen the property, so I said that if they wanted some, they would just have to come and get it.

She stated that she would be glad to have some and thanked me for the gesture. I told her to come on over. When she arrived, it was dark out so she couldn't really see the property where we were having these pig roasts she had been hearing about. I didn't want the spaghetti to get cold, so I took it to her van, put it inside on the floor, said "I hope you enjoy it." As I started to walk away. It dawned on me that I had just made a total fool of myself.

I felt very awkward. It was probably because I thought that she was cute and I felt that I had blown it on my first impression. As I was walking away, she jumped out of her van and said, "So this is the property that everyone has been talking about where you have the pig roasts." That broke the ice. The conversation became easier after that.

The next day, I texted her asking if she wanted to be on my Scripture text list I had been sending out every morning for several years. She said "yes," as long as I would be on her prophecy list. Of course, we shared a mutual interest of spreading the Word, so we struck up a friendly relationship.

A few weeks later my oldest son Jacob came to visit and ended up going to church with me. There was a fellowship meal after the service. It appeared that Beth was alone and looking for someone to sit with, so I asked her to join us. She agreed. When people were leaving, Jacob told me "I sure do wish I had a girl who looked at me the way Beth looked at you." I wondered why he would say that. I had not noticed anything special, and I don't think she intended to do anything special, but Jacob had noticed something.

Jacob continued the conversation on our ride home. "Dad, you have been alone for a long time. Mom is remarried, so why don't you open yourself up to love again?" I smiled but I told him it had been twelve years since his mother and I had split up. God would have to put a lightbulb over her head and say "Hey, Dummy. Here she is!" before I would consider being in another relationship. Remarriage was one of the furthest things from my mind. I did not want to risk another painful loss.

Even though I didn't want to think about it, I realized that my sons did not want to see me living alone. They wanted me to find love again. I knew that Beth had all the attributes I would have been looking for in a woman. She loved the Lord and worshipped Him with great passion. I was attracted to that aspect of her relationship with God because I could see that it was deep. I mustered the courage and decided to ask her out, but needed to seek wise counsel before doing it.

We had a dedication of a newly remodeled room and the hanging of another cross in the New Holland facility of The Potter's House. I had taken the job of building crosses for all the houses for The Potter's House Ministry. It was a passion for me as I carried in my heart that vision of the cross I had seen in that prison cell. The work of the cross of Christ had become part of who I was. Most of the Board members were there. It had been quite a task to turn this old garage into a workable meeting room with a bathroom, and I had been part of the process. After the ceremony, I asked Lloyd if we could talk. We stopped at a restaurant on the way home.

I was so nervous. I explained to Lloyd that I wanted Beth to know that I respected her; this was not a ploy. I was seeking to know if this was in line with God's will for either of our lives at this point. First and foremost, I wanted to go into it as a man of integrity and treat her with respect. If I was going to do this at all, it would be for the purpose of finding a partner to share my life with. I honestly think that both Beth and I were at a point in life where we both knew we didn't want drama and family problems. We both seemed comfortable with each other as we sensed we were in the same place with these issues. Lloyd affirmed my intentions.

My next step was to call Beth. After a little small talk, I asked her if she wanted to go out to dinner. The space between my question and her "yes," seemed like an hour, but I suppose it was only a brief moment. After she agreed, I made arrangements to pick her up and we went to Longhorn Steakhouse for dinner. We had such a wonderful time. I felt that I could be open about my past and not try to put on a front. Alas, I finally felt like it was okay to love again.

As we finished dinner, I really didn't feel like taking her home, but surely did not want to give her the wrong impression or do anything inappropriate. As we approached the exit to her place, I asked her if she wanted to go for a ride. She was in favor. We ended up driving about fifty miles up toward my old stomping grounds in Pottstown and stopped for coffee before starting back. I promised to have her home by 10:00 and I had every intention of keeping my promise, but I was really enjoying her company as she was mine.

From there we started dating. I continued to ask God if this was what He wanted for me. I wanted to know if God would bless the relationship, since we were both divorced. We saw life through a totally different lens than most of the married couples we knew. I searched the Scriptures and found some pretty firm stuff about God's view on divorce. I had mixed feelings about pursuing a new marriage when my first attempt had not succeeded. I had to ask myself: "Does God approve of divorce?" The answer was clear that He does not. In fact, the Bible says, "'I hate divorce,' says the Lord" (Malachi 2:16). Did I approve of divorce even though I had been through one? Of course not. I hated divorce, too!

As I reasoned with God, I began to feel more settled about the possibility of remarriage. Finally, over Easter weekend in 2015 I asked Beth if she would be willing to get up at 3:30 a.m. to go up to French Creek and watch the sunrise with me. God had spoken to me in many deep and profound ways in that place, so I thought it would be awesome for her to experience the presence of God with me there. I anticipated a glorious sunrise, but it was a bit cloudy when we arrived. Nevertheless, we sat in my truck and beheld one of the most amazing orchestrations of God's sovereignty that either one of us has ever experienced. We still talk about it to this day.

The clouds were moving across the sky and the earth seemed to be slowly moving in the opposite direction. It created a sense that we were all alone in the universe and watching a terrestrial movement. We could sense the rotation of the earth. We were somehow part of witnessing this dance of the world in God's galaxy of creation. It was as if God wanted to reveal Himself to us in a strange and wonderful way for this moment in time. Shortly after the sun came up, I asked Beth to walk down to the water with me beside Hopewell Lake. I got down on one knee and asked her to marry me. She said "Yes!"

I still wonder if our pastor friends intentionally set us up, or if God used them even though they were not aware of it. Either way, it was a huge blessing. Beth and I have been married for an amazing and wonderful six years. "Thank you, Papa, for bringing this wonderful woman into my life to walk out this journey of faith and to experience the gifts of home and family once again when I thought it would never be possible."

As we planned the wedding for November of that same year, Beth and I prayed that we would be accepted in the church we attended and could become members even as a divorced and remarried couple. I explained to the pastor and the bishop, who were also my dear friends, that I had earlier abandoned all hopes of ever marrying again. However, after deeply seeking for God's word on this matter. I had come to a place of peace about marrying Beth. I had never signed the divorce papers that my previous wife served to me, and I remained single for twelve years. My ex-wife had chosen to remarry, so I felt released from that relationship and had the blessing of my children to move on and find love again.

The crossroad between convictions and the view of being single for the rest of one's life is a difficult place to stand. I received counsel and sound instruction from people who understand the grace of God and the power of God to heal brokenness. Restoration is possible. I would challenge anyone who has suffered the pain and devastation of divorce to seek counsel from those who God has put in your life before thinking about another covenant relationship with someone. Be prepared for the differing opinions that will come out of your church body and be open to discuss and pray with those in leadership as to whether or not such a step is right for you.

Some very unique circumstances surrounded my proposal to Beth. I had read in the archives of the life of John Potts that he had proposed to his wife Ruth Savage approximately 265 years earlier on Easter weekend at French Creek. In a way, we were re-enacting history. That made it very special for both of us. It honored my heritage, and was also a signature on an event in history that was acted out again in the year 2015. We like to go back and revisit that very special moment. It has all the hallmarks of a timeless love story with God Himself writing the script. No one could deny His signature on the events.

The Spirit of the Lord was so strong in my life at that time. I felt that He was, in some strange and beautiful way, organizing and strategically putting the puzzle pieces of my life together. I was not the master of my own destiny. There seemed to be a purpose that I could not yet comprehend but I could sense God's Spirit writing this story across the pages of the annals of my life. There was a sense of something glorious about to unfold; I just had to stay the course and watch it.

Looking back over my life, I see many times when there was a divine signature on what was happening even though things seemed to be in total disarray. I didn't have to see God to know that

He was there. He was in every turn of the page and every stroke of the pen. He was dictating the story—not me. There were times when I could feel His love so distinctly that I felt He would actually physically touch me.

In 1 Corinthians 2:9 it is written: "Eye has not seen, nor ear heard, nor has it entered into the heart of man the things which God has prepared for those who love Him." Surely, I had fallen in love with this God, and He had loved me since the day I was born. Even when I couldn't see it, He was always there somehow weaving a beautiful tapestry out of the threads of my every trial. Like a master builder and a divine architect, He was forging this work of art. It would not be His masterpiece if the broken dreams and the failures were not woven in. How wonderful it is to fall into the loving arms of a beautiful Father. How sound and grounded is the man who learns to abide in the presence of His all-consuming love.

I was given a gift when I met Beth. I did not deserve her. We should all be glad that God does not give us what we deserve. Because of Jesus, we receive grace instead. I am so grateful that God gave me another chance to have a sound home and a marriage to a wonderful Spirit-filled lady whom I so lovingly call my wife. I take marriage very seriously and my covenant with God even more so. My wife lives a life of passion for God as do I. We complement each other in so many beautiful ways. It is not that we never disagree or have "heated fellowship," but we always come back to our covenant with God. I enjoy being a happily married man and I am abundantly blessed. It is all by God's grace.

The Lord has wrought such a wonderful work in my heart. The things that used to drive me are in no way the things that capture my focus now. I love my God and I love my life. I love my story and I love my wife. It's true that all things do indeed work together for good for those who love the Lord; I am experiencing this more deeply with each passing year. My prayer is that my children will come to this place of complete surrender to the One Who loves them most, and they will learn to walk in that relationship in all the areas of their lives. I know it produces a harvest of righteousness for all who follow it. I pray that they receive the generational blessing of their father who had a "raptured heart" and that their children as well would walk in that same covenant of love. "As for me and my house, we will serve the Lord" (Joshua 24:15).

Beth and I have been married going on six years now and our love continues to grow for each other and the Lord. I pray that through reading my story, you have been encouraged by what God can do in the midst of all our floundering and how He can bring incredible, good out of such devastating brokenness. He is a God of redemption. He can indeed make all things new. He is a way-maker and a promise keeper. His love never fails, even when we do.

All my life I was being prepared for something. Over the years, I had a growing anticipation for what that would mean. When all I could see was my pain, it was impossible to see God. Now the pain was gone, and hope had been reborn. The awareness of a greater purpose was stirring me.

The things that used to capture my thoughts and take me into the depths of depression were gone. A new vigor had been birthed in my heart; I was seeing life through eyes that were not mine but were His. I even chased the sunrises as if I would in some way be able to catch a glimpse of His majesty. I hungered for His presence. Where was this coming from and why was I experiencing it? What was I being strengthened and prepared for, and how was it that I could almost taste His presence?

It would not be long after this that the Lord rocked my world! I was being moved at an accelerated rate toward a goal which I had all but forgotten about. For precisely this reason, I will advise you as my reader to keep a journal. It is important to record the times when the Lord is giving you a word or a vision, even if it might seem silly or impossible to comprehend. Nothing in this life happens by accident; there is no such thing as a coincidence. He is in everything, at all times, working everything for your good. If we could only grab hold of that reality and make it our own, only God can tell what level of faith and trust could be released into our lives.

God is always ready to begin a new chapter. What if your mode of relating to the world was to see it as an unfolding prophecy? What if God's promises consumed you to the point that the problems of this life could not contain your heart's desire to do His will? What would life be like if God's reality became your reality? Have you ever wondered what would have happened if you had obeyed that still small voice telling you to do something—yet you dismissed it as crazy or impossible? We serve a God of the supernatural. He is not limited to our perception of what He can do.

CHAPTER NINE

In the Eleventh Hour

My father's health continued to deteriorate after Beth and I were married. I was still running a construction business and my life was filled with helping people in recovery and volunteering at The Potter's House. In the midst of all of that, I would still take my dad a meal every night before going home to my newly-wedded wife. He was always so angry and bitter and I knew that he did not have the Lord in his life. I had been modeling the Christian walk for years and he had softened to the fact that I had indeed changed. But he was still a huge skeptic when it came to church and to people. He didn't trust anyone and would run people off his property and threaten to shoot them if they ever came back. I had dealt with this for years, but it was still a huge source of anxiety for me. We had been having Pig Roasts there for a couple of years and my dad enjoyed the camaraderie even if he didn't trust the people. It was very trying to invite people to come enjoy this property because I would always be worried that my dad would go off like a loose cannon and ruin everything. He was very unpredictable.

I would not trade anything for the years that I spent with my dad toward the end of his life, but this was one of the most trying times of my life as well. I had learned to look past the tough façade of this Korean War Veteran and see the man who had been deeply wounded by life's circumstances. Feelings of animosity that I had harbored for most of my life had vanished. Somehow, I knew that God wanted me to be right in that place. I knew that my dad loved me in his somewhat twisted perception of love, but it was the only way that he knew how to show it. Somehow, I needed to feel love from my father. I was in such great hopes that the same love of God I had experienced would soften his heart as well.

The summer before our fall wedding, I got a call from my dad one afternoon. He was unable to get out of his bed and his girlfriend was sitting in the living room unresponsive. I dropped what I was doing and rushed back to his house. Judy had passed away sitting there in the living room. I called the police and the coroner to come verify her time of death. This was tough on my dad. Judy had taken care of him for nearly twenty years. Although he had treated her badly for a good portion of that time, she stuck with him. He really never showed much emotion about her passing and I really wondered if this man's heart was so hardened that he could not feel compassion for anyone.

I realized that I was the only one he had left in this world to care for him unless my sister and I found a home for him to move into. He didn't interview well with the homes we tried due to his habit of shouting expletives. My sister and I went back and forth for a good while about who would take care of him. In the end, I was the one who walked the final miles with my dad.

During that time, he was exposed to people from my church. He even had a few visits from retired pastor, Glenn Hoover and our dear pastor Samuel Mwangi from Carpenter Church. Pastor Glenn had a kind and patient way with people and my dad liked him. Pastors had never come to visit him before as he ran most people off. It was uncanny that my Kenyan pastor, Samuel, could come see him because my day was a personified bigot. It was an act of God that he seemed receptive to talk with Pastor Samuel. On the Christmas before he passed, the church came to sing Christmas carols for him. I think he was open to church folk for the first time in his life, and he experienced love from the community of faith around him.

One Sunday morning I was sitting in church in a row close to the front and out of nowhere I heard my dad's voice. "Anyone see Rob?" he yelled. He had gotten on his electric wheelchair and rode from his decrepit, old cabin in the woods for at least two whole miles to see what this church was all about! He was nearly deaf and very loud, but he was at church! He had told pastor Glenn that he would never step foot in that church. But there he was, big as life, driving himself in an electric wheelchair to the church!

For the next month or two he would show up at church quite regularly. Everyone was so nice to him. He spoke loudly and was still rude—but no one paid attention to that. They would just tell him, "Glad to see you, Mr. Weatherholtz." I think they killed him with kindness. I began to see a change in my dad's heart.

One day when I was taking him something to eat, he looked at me and said, "You know son, they are nice people and maybe I was wrong about them." I just smiled, wishing he had found this out years before. Things may have been so different if someone would have just shown him Christian love and acceptance. Maybe he could have found healing from all that pain.

In the days ahead there were frequent trips to the VA Hospital in Lebanon. I spent a lot of time talking to people about his care and seeking for a visiting nurse. It seemed like there was not much hope for him to achieve a level of self-care that was conducive to independent living, and we were concerned about him being alone all the time. Some folks from the church would stop by now and then to check in on him while I was working. Beth once went to make him some eggs for lunch. When she was in the kitchen, he started yelling at her telling her if she didn't show her face, he was going to shoot her! My goodness, he was a mess!

Beth proceeded to go straight in his room and set him straight on how he was to address her. In some ways it was hilarious, and in some ways, it was really sad. He could not get out of bed to see who came in the door and when he knew someone was there, he would get scared and threaten to shoot them if they didn't show themselves.

It was really rather frightening that my dad kept loaded guns in his bedroom even though he wasn't even supposed to have guns. Years before, when we had lived in Middletown, Pennsylvania, my dad had an altercation with a police officer who had come because my dad had beaten my mother. He took a gun from the police officer so they ruled that he could never own a gun again. As with most rules, my dad believed this one didn't apply to him. He was indeed one of a kind. If I were to tell all the stories, I could probably fill a whole book!

With Judy gone, he found himself alone with failing health and felt scared and vulnerable for the first time in his life. I really felt bad for him, but he had scared off most anyone who ever tried to help him. He was fiercely opposed to being put in a home. All his life he had the illusion of being in control; now he was helpless. My sister Robin was always working behind the scenes to make sure his bills were paid and he kept his medical appointments. But she lived twenty miles away, so all of the hands-on work was up to me.

Even though my dad was a mean old man to a lot of people, he still was a Korean War Veteran and had served his country. He was wounded in battle and sent home to recover from his injuries. He deserved some respect for his service to our country. I will never forget a sticker that he had on the back of one of his pick-up trucks that said, "For those who fought for it, freedom has a taste that the protected will never know." I never forgot that sticker. It reminded me that my dad had fought for our country.

As weird as this may sound, I loved my dad and I knew that he loved me, even though it didn't look like the traditional or family model for love. I honored him in his last days even when he was less than honorable in his behaviors with those around him. In some ways it was respect and in others it was my call to honor my father and mother as the Bible tells me to do. I am so glad I walked the last few miles with this soldier that never really came home from the war. Violence and adversity, such as that which he experienced in the service, seemed to be a normal and acceptable way of life for my dad. But all this didn't make for a very good husband or father figure in my life and family.

I suspect my dad had been taught that showing feelings or emotions was a sign of weakness. How sad it is for many of our men to be trained as battle hardened soldiers in war, yet never be able to transition into being good husbands and fathers. How tough it is on the next generation of kids that grow up in the socially disconnected aftermath of war. Thank God for Jesus Christ and thank God for grace and mercy and forgiveness; the world would be such a cold and dark place without it. God has the power to break down all those walls and to heal the most hardened hearts if we only trust Him to do so.

My dad was the youngest of seven boys. He told me how he and his brothers used to fight and how they used to pick on him until he came home from the war. After that, they realized that they couldn't mess with him anymore. He certainly had his own unique set of challenges and his own demons to battle as well, but he forged his way through life the only way he knew how. When I could see my father as a man who had endured a lot then I was able to look past the hurt that he had caused me and feel empathy for what he had become.

Upon visiting with my uncles, especially my uncle Charlie, I had glimpses into the environment they must have grown up in. Uncle Charlie also had an unbridled tongue, and his disposition was much like my dad's. They used to compete to see who could make the most money. It's a shame because we don't take anything to the grave with us. I once heard a saying, "I never saw a U-Haul behind a hearse." It is so true. The Lord has given us blessings to steward while we are here but in the end it all belongs to Him. He will give it to whomever He pleases.

Beth and I, my sister Robin and those close to us in the church walked those last days with my dad. In January 2016 he became very ill and ended up in the Emergency Room at Lancaster General Hospital. They told him he was living on only 10 percent of his kidneys and his heart was failing as well. He had to come to terms with his own mortality and we all knew that the end was near. They said they could not operate on his kidneys because his heart would fail, and they could not operate on his heart because his kidneys would fail; he was in a no-win situation.

My sister and I started to formulate a plan for his burial as there was very little that the doctors could do. We had to decide what responsibilities each of us would have in carrying out his last wishes. I already knew that I would be the one to sift through the ten thousand items that he had accumulated. He was an extreme hoarder and never threw anything away. He said that everything had a memory attached to it. We visited him many times during those last days. I continued to pray that in some miraculous way he would make peace with God and accept Jesus before he went on from this life.

One Sunday, Beth and I went directly to the hospital to see dad after the service. When the elevator doors for his floor slid open, there stood my dear friend and spiritual father, Lloyd Hoover. Beth and I looked at each other and somehow, we knew that God was in this. We all proceeded to dad's room and when we arrived, he was happy to see us.

As we took turns talking to him, I felt the Lord prompt me to go stand beside him and tell dad that I loved him and that I was concerned about his eternal place of rest. As I approached his bedside, I had an overwhelming burden for this man's soul. I approached him and said, "Dad, I want to tell you that I love you, and I want to ask you something. Don't you want to forgive the people in your life that hurt you and be forgiven for the people that you may have hurt along life's way?" He looked at me and began to tear up. Beth began to pray and then she shared some scriptures on forgiveness and how important it was for us to make peace on this side of eternity.

My dad then began to pour out some of the things he had witnessed when in Korea and started confessing how he hardened himself toward people because of those experiences. He shared some very graphic and horrific things. He had to unburden himself from those memories. The more he talked about the war, the more emotional he became! What a burden this man had been carrying all these years. How it held him in bondage to bitterness and mistrust. My dad also stated that he knew he had done some things wrong and that he wanted to be forgiven.

Right then, Lloyd Hoover stepped up and asked him if he wanted to accept Jesus as his Savior. For the first time, I saw my dad humble himself and say "Yes, I want to accept Jesus!" Lloyd walked him through a prayer of repentance and salvation. Right there on his death bed, my dad made peace with God and the world he had known! It was such a holy moment. I don't think that Beth, I or Lloyd will ever forget what God did in the eleventh hour of my dad's life. We left there that day with a burden lifted. I especially felt so elated because for years I had talked to my dad about Jesus and all he would say was that he wasn't going to fall for those "religious people's" God. He would call them hypocrites. But here he was, with no hope left in this world, gaining eternal hope for his life in the next. It was so good!

The hospital bills kept coming and my sister Robin finally decided that it was in his best interest to be taken to a nursing home called Hamilton Arms Center. However, they were asking for more than he could pay without needing to surrender his property and bank accounts to Medicare. My sister tried everything she could to find him reasonable care and she finally found a place called Evergreen Estates Assisted Living Community in Lancaster. It was affordable enough that we could work with them in taking care of my dad.

The morning they were supposed to transport him to the new facility, we showed up early to fill out the paperwork. Dad was brought in an ambulance in the afternoon. He was ash gray and his color was gone. I could tell he was slipping away. As soon as they got him into his room, we called for a medic. They came and took his vitals and discovered that his blood pressure had bottomed out, so they had to rush him to the Lancaster General Hospital. My sister followed the ambulance to the hospital and told me she would call me as soon as he stabilized. That was never to come.

My dad died on that chilly February day in 2016 in the emergency room at the Lancaster General Hospital, just three months after Beth and I got married. My sister called me as he was slipping away. When I reached the hospital, he had already passed. My sister, brother-in-law and I got to say our goodbyes to him in the hospital ER. We cried and hugged his lifeless body. I whispered to him that he could go be at peace now and the war was finally over.

That next weekend we had a funeral in the cemetery at Zion Lutheran Church in Leola, Pennsylvania. I called some friends of mine, one from the Honor Guard and another who served in the Air Force, to ask if they would help me to give him a military burial. They both knew me from the recovery circles I had been involved in, so they were honored to be a part of my dad's last wishes. The funeral was so moving as they did a six-gun salute for a fallen soldier and presented me with an American flag to commemorate my dad's service. My dear brother who married Beth and I, Pastor Samuel Mwangi, facilitated the funeral.

Afterwards, we all went back to the church for a memorial service at our church. I read my dad's eulogy. I depicted him as a young man who at eighteen years of age was flown halfway across the world and dropped off in a war zone in Korea. He had struggled with the memories all his life and it made it hard for him to live a normal life. I honored his memory and told the story of how he had accepted the Lord in the eleventh hour. I thanked him for being my father. The whole town knew him for his cantankerous nature and his service to our country. The newspaper obituary said that he was a colorful character in the Brownstown area for many years. A lot of people from the recovery community and the faith community supported us.

Several days later, I went back to the property and started to sift through the thousands of trinkets that my dad had collected over the years. I relived a lot of his experiences through all this memorabilia. There were Harley Davidson memorabilia and old WWII helmets and cast-iron Hubli statues of the Planters Peanut man and Aunt Jemima… the list never seemed to end. I was getting deeper insight into my dad's likes and dislikes. There were seventeen vehicles on the property, three motorcycles, various mopeds and a ton of mowers and riding mowers. There was also a collection of old tools and drills and saws dating back at least thirty years; he had saved them all. He indeed was a professional hoarder. I was going to be the one to organize and pull together an auction.

It was still winter and there was a ton of work that needed to be done. It was hard for me to go through that house and experience all his memories. It was a deep journey of my soul at the same time as it was bringing closure to many chapters of my life which had been tumultuous for at least fifty years. Now it was coming to an end. Before my dad passed away, he pulled me aside and told me that he wanted to leave me this property in his will because I had come there so many times, cleaned it up, done renovations and built decks. I felt very blessed that he would do that but by the same token I was overwhelmed with the task of cleaning the place.

While I was going through the belongings, I stumbled across a picture that I had drawn and sent to him years before. It was the picture of several houses positioned on his property and it was titled Still Waters Retreat. I had wanted to inspire him to do something with this beautiful property along the Conestoga River. He always laughed when I came to him with these ideas and would say, "I hope you make a lot of money and fix this place all up when I'm gone."

That was such a prophetic word. It seemed like an impossible undertaking to actually get the property in a place that something could be done with it. It would have been a huge expense to increase the quality of the cabins that were on the property or turn them into year-round dwellings. My dad had lived in the largest cabin on the property for thirty-plus years and even that was supposed to be a seasonal dwelling by code. Somehow, he managed to make it work without any pushback from the township or local authorities.

It happened that a friend of mine, Mel Horst, who was an elder at Carpenter Church where we attended, had a friend who was an auctioneer. He guided us through the process of cataloging organizing everything for the auction block. It was a massive undertaking and I worked round the clock it seemed, cleaning and fixing up the vehicles so that they would at least be presentable enough to sell. Some of them had been out in the weather for years and I could hear my dad's voice saying how he didn't want to sell this car or that truck because he paid so much for it when he bought it. Little did he consider that they had been out in the weather for years and things were rotted out; the rubber on the sidewalls of the tires were splitting and dry-rotting.

During this time of transition, I had time to reflect on the life of a man who had been my father and how very little I really knew about him. There was so much of his side of the family that I never really got to know due to my parents splitting up when I was a young man. There were times I loved him and times that I hated him for ripping our family apart, but I understood how life must have been for him. The Lord had dealt with me in all those secret places of my heart and now I was faced with sifting through a lifetime of lost heritage and a multitude of emotions. I relived so much devastation and so many missed opportunities to really get to know my dad and what the war had stolen from him.

I can't even say how many times I would break down in tears over the lost years as I was forging my way through this project. I would catch glimpses of the moments of clarity he would have, and the brief and fleeting moments when we actually did feel like family. Even though he was gone I still yearned for the love and approval of the father that I felt I had barely known. My emotions were torn and my thoughts were scattered. I don't know if my family members knew how hard it was for me emotionally to take on this massive task. All I know is that somehow God was tearing down the walls of my heart in the process and preparing me for things that only He could have foreknown.

After a couple of months of preparation, that day finally arrived. Many people showed up for the auction. Those who knew my dad and those who followed auctions for a living came to see the wares that were on display. As things started to disappear, I had a sense of closure. A vision began to emerge, one that I had always known but found difficult to believe. It was a beautiful oasis of a property. I grew deeply grateful for the loving support of family and my church, for the close ties to my community that I had established, and the love and support from my sister Robin who had stuck by me through thick and thin when walking those last days with my dad.

One thing that my dad did was to try and eliminate any squabbling among his children over who would receive what. We all wanted the same thing, peace in the process as we grieved the loss of our father and peace with each other in the aftermath of his passing. Too many times there is division in a family when one person receives more than the other in the wishes of the departed. I was truly thankful that this was not the case with my sister and me. In light of the many years of our strained relationship, I was not sure that He would even include me in his last will and testament. My sister was to receive all his cash and liquidated assets and I was to receive the property that I had put so much into over the years.

I was always able to forge out a pretty good living for myself through the remodeling and construction business that I had established, so I didn't feel I had to depend on anybody. But I was blessed to know that my family was always there for me even if we were all going in different directions. It dawned on me that if my dad had passed away three days later, everything would have been a loss. Medicare would have taken all his assets and he would have spent the rest of his days in a rest home without a thing to pass on to his children. This is a sad fact for many people who fall ill in their later years. The medical bills pile up and the high cost of health care eat all the assets a person has worked so hard for. I'm sure they feel horrible because they intended to leave something behind for their children. I honestly believe that my dad's passing three days prior to him losing everything was an act of divine providence. Some things in life have no other explanation other than that they were orchestrated by divine providence and not thought up by any man.

CHAPTER TEN

The Big Jigsaw Puzzle in the Sky

After we were married, Beth and I had moved into her apartment. I kept my camper over at the property I had inherited from my dad and became the caretaker of this retreat of sorts. From time to time, I would go there to pray and seek the Lord. Beth and I would have conversations about what we wanted to do with this property. Did we want to demolish the cottages, build a home here and keep doing what we had been doing?

We had another pig roast the year after my father passed away. The atmosphere at this event was so powerful! We ended up doing several baptisms in the river behind the property that day. The worship was constant. I heard God's voice say clearly, "Finish the work that I had started in you." It was such a profound word. I went to my camper and sat to listen for that still small voice. I began to read in Psalms 23 "He makes me to lie down in green pastures: he leadeth me beside the still waters and He restores my soul."

All of the sudden, as I gazed over the meadow and the river, it hit me in full color. I was not just reading the scripture, but I was living right in the middle of it! In some miraculous way, I had become part of this scripture! The last time I had experienced anything like that, I had been living in Pottstown. Now God was speaking to me in that same manner all over again. It was as if God was crossing over from His realm of existence to ours and opening my eyes to see something beautiful and wonderful that He had known and planned for my life all along. It blew my mind and melted my heart.

From then on, the vision and I became one. At first, I shared it only with my wife, but the vision was not meant for me alone. I sought the Lord with a fervor as to what He wanted me to do. I pressed in and contended with Him every morning as if I were Jacob wrestling with an angel. When God spoke to me in this way it was always followed by a major shift in energy and a drastically enhanced spiritual fervor for the things that were of Him.

The work of His Holy Spirit had enraptured my heart. A divine mission had been set before me to accomplish. My focus on what He was calling me to do was laser-sharp. As I contended with the Lord, it was as if this big jigsaw puzzle in the sky was coming together in my mind and my heart. It was as if my whole life had been preparing me for what He was bringing me to in the present. It all tied together so uniquely that no man on earth could have planned it. This had the signature of the Almighty God. This work was His mission for my life.

Soon thereafter, as I was praying in the spirit in my camper, He began to show me times in my life that He was with me even when I had no idea that He was present. When I was a child and there was so much abuse in my family, He was preparing me to become a minister to those who were broken. When I had run away to Florida, He was preparing me to minister to the prodigal sons of this world about a prodigal Father's love over their lives. All this happened when I felt like I was abandoned and all alone in this world, yet He was right there, protecting me, guiding me, and providing for me.

These waves of His providence over my life seemed to cleanse and comfort me. They had the power to renew my strength and mount me up on eagle's wings as it says in Isaiah 40:31. The scriptures were indeed alive and active. I could see and feel them driving my every ambition and lining them up with His ambitions for me.

I learned to abide under the shadow of His wings and fall into a deep love relationship with Him. I knew that He had His hand on my life and I had nothing to fear. I had everything to live for and a prophecy to fulfill.

As I sat in that camper, I began to draw a picture. Suddenly it dawned on me that this was the vision God had given me so many years ago when I was in that prison cell in Lancaster County prison! Oh, my Lord! My sweet, sweet Jesus! You were always there! In that prison cell, You came to me and showed me the reality of your power and love to rip through the atmosphere and send demons fleeing! You were there to cut through bars of iron, penetrate concrete walls and pierce the atmosphere with Your sovereign presence! You silenced the principalities of darkness and clothed your child with peace in the presence of my enemies! Surely there is none like You in all the earth, my Lord, my Rock, my Savior!

The picture that I found myself drawing for this piece of inherited land had three houses. God had told me nearly thirteen years before that He was going to bring forth a center for the healing of the broken and addicted and create a revival that would impact the lives of many. Vividly detailed information was now being downloaded into my mind and heart day after day. This was much like my experience at the Schuylkill River as I could see the beginning and the end of the vision all at once just like I saw Pottstown being torn down and being built back up.

"But how, Lord?" I would ask. "How on earth was this supposed to ever be realized? I was just a man on a meager budget. Tearing down the cabins would take a massive amount of money, let alone putting up new buildings. At times I thought I was just imagining all this myself.

I had to lay down my limited view of what was possible and trust that if this was from God, He would open the opportunity for it to happen. It would have to be a total walk in faith and manifest in such a way that no human being could take the credit. I would be tested to see if I had the courage to pursue such a seemingly impossible task. Proverbs 3:5-6 says, "Trust the Lord with all your heart and lean not to your own understanding, but in all your ways acknowledge Him and He will direct your paths."

I had to literally abandon the realm of human possibilities and embrace a vision that seemed impossible. I didn't have to understand it; I just had to "trust the Lord." I drew up a plan, wrote a proposal, and determined to take it to The Potter's House Board of Directors, of which I was a member. The vision was in line with the heart of God in rescuing the broken and afflicted as is written in Isaiah 61.

"The Spirit of the Lord has anointed me to proclaim good news to the poor. He has sent me to bind up the brokenhearted, to proclaim freedom for the captives and release from darkness for the prisoners, to proclaim the year of the Lord's favor and the day of vengeance of our God, to comfort all who mourn, and provide for those who grieve in Zion- to bestow on them a crown of beauty instead of ashes, the oil of joy instead of mourning, and a garment of praise instead of despair. They will be called oaks of righteousness, a planting of the Lord for the display of His splendor. They will rebuild the ancient ruins and restore the places long devastated; they will renew the ruined cities that have been devastated for generations."

This was it! It was Jesus' heart to redeem, restore and revive that which was lost and in ruins. This work lined up with the heart of Christ and His purposes for coming to Earth. I had to muster the courage to pursue this noble call and press in and trust the Lord at levels I had never imagined.

This was the scripture Jesus read in the synagogue in Nazareth as He spoke about Himself and what He came to do. He really shocked the religious leaders when He said, "Today, in your hearing, the scriptures are fulfilled." They did not believe they were standing in the presence of the Messiah. It was too much for those who were raised under the law of Moses. They were the descendants of Abraham, right? They had taught the people for over a thousand years, and all of the sudden this son of Joseph the carpenter comes along and claims to be the chosen Messiah of God spoken of throughout the scriptures. How could this be?

It's amazing how, today, religious people can be so skeptical about someone who carries a prophetic anointing instead of embracing the gift. Not much has changed in many religious denominations from the time when Jesus walked this earth in regard to embracing the prophetic gifts. I pray that this book may open the eyes of many a reader to the fact that it is God who determines prophets. It is God who sends messengers amongst us even today. All the religious training in the world does not qualify someone to be a prophet. God does not choose those who are qualified, but He qualifies those who are chosen.

I mustered up the courage to present this vision to the Board of Directors at the Potter's House Ministry. I felt that they would either tell me I was crazy or embrace the vision and trust God to make it happen. At the next board meeting I spoke up and described the vision of God establishing a healing center on the property that my dad owned I had while in prison thirteen years before. I expected these men and women to tell me that it was a fine idea but there was no way it could happen financially.

Conversation was stirred up amongst the Board members. Talk slowly began to emerge about whether this was even a possibility. Looking back, I have to laugh about the time when I took the chairman of the board and dear friend Jay Mylin to see the property. After hearing the vision, I remember how he smiled at me as if to be polite while in the back of his mind was thinking "This guy is just a dreamer." The property had old cabins on it that were all but condemned. It would be a massive undertaking to even get the land ready for building.

By the next board meeting, the idea was adopted by these men and women of faith and planning began. "Was this really happening?" I asked myself. "Could God be using me to fulfill this vision? Had He planned it all along?" I began to see my life and every intricate part so uniquely preparing me for the tasks ahead of me.

I remembered how God had led me, by divine providence, into a relationship with Navy Seals in Virginia Beach. I remembered how He shaped my attitude to believe that nothing was impossible and giving up was not an option. He was teaching me how to persevere and training me for what He knew was ahead. He used the brokenness in my family to prepare me for the healing that I was to bring. How do I know this was of God? This was certainly not the plan I had for my own life; it was the plan of God. I can take no credit.

God gave me discernment into the brokenness of the human heart so that I could see the work of the enemy in people's lives and attack it with the goodness of God. The same restorative work that Jesus came to do was what I was being called to carry on. How honored I felt to be a part of His kingdom, doing the work of my Lord and impacting the lives of many. I believe the healing of hearts changes the course of generations for His honor and glory.

This could not have been a work of man. Even meeting the members of the Board of Directors of The Potter's House had to be divinely orchestrated. God brought us together as a team of uniquely qualified men and women to partner in the culmination of this vision. Throughout the 20-plus years of The Potter's House Ministry, before I was involved, my dear friend and spiritual father Lloyd Hoover had it on his heart to do this work.

Each member of the Board had unique training in different areas. Jay Mylin, the Chairman, was a long-time member of the Manheim Brethren in Christ Church along with John Wagner. John was an incredible bridge-builder between the faith community and the business community. Bud Roda was a long-time volunteer chaplain at the Lancaster County Prison and was responsible for taking me to The Potter's House as a student some fifteen years before. John Leaman was an influential pastor and successful businessman in the Lancaster County area. Lanny and Debbie Millette were also on the Board, Lanny being the Ministry Director of The Potter's House when we started and Debbie having so many administrative skills that I can't even name them all. God had put together a league of extraordinary people for the task He had set before us. Each one of us would play an intricate part of this master plan. Without the talents of all together, it could not have worked.

John Miller, a brother to John Wagner's wife Joyce, was called in to create a capital campaign. We called it "Captivity to Destiny," which is really the story of my life in a nutshell. We spent the better part of a year planning and counting the cost. Now we look back and laugh about how we thought that we could fix up those cabins and use them as group homes.

We called some builders from the plain community to assess the possibility of fixing up the existing buildings. They found structural problems and all kinds of issues, as they had been built for seasonal use only. Our plain community friends had a group that was addressing issues of addiction in their community. I would not have thought that such a clean living and down to earth people could have addiction issues, but they did. We would join their awareness meetings and support one another in the training and equipping of families and leaders when dealing with the issues of addiction.

They were joined in heart to our vision of developing a faith-based center for recovery. My heart goes out to the plain community with a sincere debt of gratitude for their willingness to embrace this work. This whole movement allowed us to set aside our differences and work together to achieve the common goal of saving the lost and bringing restoration to individuals and families.

One day after meeting with the Amish builders, I started to discuss this with my wife Beth. She just looked at me and said, "I think God wants to tear it all down and erect new buildings on the property." I immediately saw in front of me my own limitations, both financially and physically. This was a massive undertaking. I was overwhelmed. How on earth would it ever be possible?

I was reminded of Philippians 4:13 which says, "I can do all things through Christ who gives me strength." That was it! I was looking at my human limitations and seeing all the challenges. I needed to understand that it would not be me who would be building this. I needed to trust that as I offered myself to the Lord, He would provide the wisdom, strength and resources. I spoke with Lloyd Hoover, and he felt the same way. It would take an act of God. Although we did not know it at that time, that is exactly what God had in mind.

We agreed as the Board to search the possibilities of creating this facility. The first step was to get the approval of the Township to build such a facility off the beaten path but also very close to a residential area. We scheduled a zoning commission hearing to discuss the possibility of this venture and prayed fervently that they would see value for the community in building this center. In the meeting, we spoke about how it could reduce crime and help community members join with local churches. We all wanted to see sick and struggling individuals get well and heal their individual lives as well as their families.

We had no idea that some members of the zoning board also desired to see captives set free. Many were in favor of the idea. I stood up at the end of the hearing and asked the township to not only approve this facility but to also come alongside us and embrace this work for the restoration of lives and the ongoing health and growth of our community.

I left that meeting feeling good about the possibility of getting the zoning board's backing. About two weeks later, I received a call that the project was approved. I fell to my knees and began to cry. I couldn't believe that the pieces of this big jigsaw puzzle in the sky were being favored by both God and men! I felt the hand of God and the anointing of His Holy Spirit on every part of the process. I remembered the jail cell experience when God first gave me the vision for all that He was preparing me to do.

The first major hurdle was over, but there were still many challenges ahead. The next major hurdle was the need for us to purchase the adjacent property in order to fulfill the right of way requirements. It was owned by a retired narcotics officer out of the Bronx, New York. This could have shut down the whole project, but I was able to get in touch with the oldest son of the owner and ask him some questions. I researched the rights of families of properties in New York in cases where there was no will and found that, in this situation, their son Joey was indeed qualified to hold Power of Attorney.

The lot had been abandoned for at least ten years. It was a mess. Vines were growing inside the run-down cabins on the property. We worked with Joey to legally secure the Power of Attorney status while trusting the Lord to bless the capital campaign so we could get funds to purchase the property. Even believing it would be possible was a stretch. We had to involve attorneys from both Pennsylvania and New York to work through this process. Lloyd Hoover worked tirelessly with the lawyers while I helped to raise funds.

Finally in April 2017, after a year of painstaking effort, we were able to work out the interstate details and raise enough money to purchase the Fiorini property! This was miracle number two.

We had started a capital campaign to raise two million dollars for the building of this facility and the longer-term purpose of sustaining the ministry as well as the development of a women's facility. In approximately eighteen months we had raised $850,000. This demonstrated amazing support from the surrounding community and favor from God. This was miracle number three as we had started with nothing toward raising the funds for this project.

I made an agreement with The Potter's House Board that they could purchase my property for much less than the fair market value and in exchange build a director's house on the site for me and Beth. This was a win—win situation for everyone. In turn I was seeing a God-breathed vision come to life.

The next challenge was to get the right of way going into the property with the adjoining businesses and the water and sewer issues needed to support eighteen people on the site. The existing well could only supply seasonal cabins with a flow of water for minimal showers and cooking capacity. We had the water tested and found questionable iron and coliform content. We had three options: to move the well and dig another one, to dig deeper in search of a fresh water spring, or to tap into the township water supply which was over three hundred feet away. The latter choice would have an astronomical price tag and ongoing water bills.

As God's providence would have it, we called a local well drilling company in to dig a deeper well close to the existing well. At around five hundred feet they found a spring of fresh water that would be more than sufficient for our needs. It dawned on me that the Lord knew all along that the water was there and that we would find it. It is much like how we live our lives; sometimes we just have to dig a little deeper to find a fresh reserve of what the Lord has for us. So many things that are true in the spiritual realm are also true in the natural realm. This was playing itself out on many different levels in this project; every step seemed to have a divine lesson attached to it.

Our surveyor had said it could take five to ten years to get all the approvals needed for a facility with this many challenges. Yet, less than two years into the project, we were finding favor with everyone involved. In Luke 18:27, Jesus referred to salvation and told those who were with Him that "What is impossible for man is very possible with God." In our case, many people came to the Lord because of what we were attempting to accomplish. This was also right smack in the middle of the nationwide opioid crisis that had taken the lives of over seventy thousand Americans the year before. This was more than the sixty-two thousand who were lost over the course of twenty years in the Vietnam War.

Next, we had to get the land development plan approved. This meant having all of the houses positioned on the property in such a way that they would maintain the proper distance from the property lines and each other. This was the most daunting task as there were six lots on this property. All the existing boundary lines had to be removed and the entire property deeded again as one lot for a year-round occupancy approval. All of this was contingent on the water and sewer being appropriate and the logistical hookups meeting code for a group home facility. This was a painstaking process. As it went along, we were confronted with challenge after challenge that required perseverance beyond the normal realm of human resolve.

I was wearing several different hats at one time during this process. As I look back, I can see that God was carrying me through uncharted waters. I was doing part-time ministry for The Potter's House, running a construction business on the side, and assisting the project manager we had recruited out of the Amish community, Elmer Fisher. Elmer's brothers, Mel and Dan Fisher, both had exterior remodeling businesses and were part of the Amish Awareness Committee that had been formed out of concern for their youth and the community's well being.

Elmer and I seemed to have a kindred spirit from the moment we met. God was using us to break down the walls of division between the recovery community and the deeply-rooted faith community in Lancaster County. It was becoming a kingdom partnership between two worlds that rarely worked together. God was tearing down the walls of diversity as His people joined hands to bring healing and restoration to individuals, families and even communities. Somehow, God was behind the scenes pulling all the strings and lining up each individual in this divinely orchestrated dance that broke down even cultural barriers that had long been in place.

This level of Holy Spirit-driven enthusiasm could be the catalyst for revival on all levels of society. God uses tragedies to bring about massive shifts in revival between people of differing cultures. Look at 9/11 when the Twin Towers came crashing down. People from all over the country worked together as one to comfort and restore the lives that were devasted in this event. Then there was hurricane Katrina down in Louisiana and the massive outpouring of aid that came to help the devastated communities in those perilous times.

This was not a natural disaster, but a massive spiritual attack on human lives through the infiltration of the drug culture in our society. Everyone was on board with doing their part to create safe and restorative environments conducive to the preservation of human lives and the return to faith values that our country was founded upon.

We were all thrust into this spiritual warfare together. The people of God, chosen for such a time as this, had to rise up and fight back against the tactics of the enemy to steal, kill and destroy. Every life lost was someone's brother or sister, father or mother, son or daughter or dear friend. No one was exempt from the attack. The enemy was crossing the social and cultural barriers of our society at unprecedented levels. Government officials at the state level testified of the loss of their sons; everyone had been to so many unnecessary funerals.

Even I had to facilitate my oldest daughter, Jessica's funeral because of a drug overdose. It was one of the hardest things any father would have to face. It is heart-wrenching and so unnecessary. It leaves a void in the hearts of those who are left behind. The grief is beyond anything a parent should have to endure. Those who are affected carry hurt and pain with them for a long time. On every birthday and every holiday, there is that empty seat at the table. You would give anything to hold the child in your arms again and just tell them that you love them and that everything is going to be alright. But they are not there anymore. I wish that no one would ever have to endure that level of sorrow—but we live in a broken world and the Enemy is not going away. We must rise up for the glory of God and the sanctity of human life!

What the Enemy wanted to use to break me became fuel to fan the flames of revival. I became more driven and determined than ever to create safe outposts for those who had been wounded. We would heal and train warriors that were once oppressed by the enemy and imprisoned in their own lives of addiction for the Kingdom of God. Once a person is truly set free as I was by the finished work of the cross of Christ, they are a force to be reckoned with in the battle.

2 Corinthians 10:4 says, "For the weapons of our warfare are not of the flesh, but divinely powerful for the pulling down of strongholds." In essence we use God's mighty weapons to knock down strongholds of human reasoning and to destroy false arguments. The Lord will begin to reveal to every born-again believer the battle that they are really in, and what they are really fighting against. It's not people that we have to battle against, it is principalities and demonic strongholds in our thinking processes that keep us from seeing the reality of the power of the resurrected Jesus and the full measure of His impact on the believer's life.

The battle can come in so many forms. We can be enslaved in the practice of religious behaviors just as much as we can be ensnared by the forces of darkness that accompany drug and alcohol or sexual addiction. Many good church-going folk may be shocked to realize that they have been serving as servants of religion rather than as born-again children of their one and only Savior. Jesus came to set both the broken and those bound in religion completely free.

You can't be saved merely by being an active member of a local congregation. Our salvation comes through the sacrifice of Jesus

Christ and his shed blood for the atonement of our sins. While we are told not to forsake the gathering of the brethren, we dare not worship the church or the doctrine of men. We are called to gather at the church but to worship the Lord who established the church. This could be a revelation to those who have given their lives to do good works as a church member. It is the power of the risen Savior, not the rule of church doctrine, which sets men free.

It is a revelation to the destitute and lost to be set free from their addictions as much as it is a revelation to the soul that gets born again from a religious spirit that is not from God but from men. Jesus came to seek and save the lost. That includes the religious along with the sinner in the deceived society in which we live. It is time for a generation to wake up and enter into the fullness of this great and awesome salvation plan through Jesus. We can live out this great salvation with the same passion that Jesus showed as He willingly died on the cross to restore the relationship between God the Father and mankind.

Jesus is an equal opportunity Savior! He is not exclusive. He wants each and every one of us to come to repentance under His plan of salvation. His sacrifice alone qualifies us for this gift from God to the world. Neither our rebellion nor our religion will determine our qualification for heaven. When we stand before God, our works will be examined. Were they done for Christ or out of our own search for self-importance? Our only qualification is what we did with the great salvation that He gave us in the form of His Son. It cannot be found in the meetings we attended, the number of boards we sat on, or our religious affiliation. Only what we did with Jesus will determine our place of eternal residence.

The Bible explains this in Matthew 20:1-16:

> "For the kingdom of heaven is like a landowner who
> went out early in the morning to hire laborers for his

vineyard. Now when he had agreed with the laborers for a denarius a day, he sent them into his vineyard. And he went out about the third hour and saw others standing idle in the marketplace, and he said to them, 'You also go into the vineyard, and whatever is right I will give you.' So, they went. Again, he went out about the sixth and the ninth hour, and he did likewise. And about the eleventh hour he went out and found others standing idle and he said to them, 'Why have you been standing idle all day?'

"They said to him, 'because no one hired us.' He said to them, 'You also go into the vineyard, and whatever is right you will receive.' So, when evening had come, the landowner of the vineyard said to his steward, 'Call the laborers and give them their wages, beginning with the last to the first.' And when those came who were hired at the eleventh hour, they received a denarius.

'But when then the first came, they supposed that they would receive more; and they each received a denarius. And when they had received it, they complained against the landowner, saying, these last men have worked only one hour, and you made them equal to us that have borne the burden and the heat of the day. But he answered one of them and said, 'Friend, I am doing you no wrong. Did you not agree with me for a denarius? Take what is yours and go your way. I wish to give to this last man the same as to you. Is it not lawful for me to do what I wish with my own things? Or is your eye evil because I am good? So, the last will be first and the first will be last."

"For many are called but few are chosen" (Matthew 22:14). These are the very words of Jesus, but how often are the chosen passed over by men because of preference toward those who have labored long in the field? How many are held back because elder boards do not deem them to be as qualified as those who have labored long in faith? It would serve churches quite well to stop overlooking the called for the sake of preserving the status quo and to start allowing the Owner of the Vineyard to make the decisions on who He calls to labor in His field.

We are in a time where the lives of men and women are being snuffed out by drugs and alcohol and pandemics are raging. It's going to take more than business as usual to overcome the on-slaught of enemy attacks on an entire generation. Those whom the Lord has raised up to do battle with the elemental forces of evil in this world are not the average Sunday Christians. It is people who have been anointed to display the power and sovereignty of God. The enemy knows the weakness of the lethargy of a lukewarm society and a lukewarm church and wants to exploit those weaknesses in order to render them powerless and ineffective. We must rise up! The spiritual warfare going on in this generation is at levels we have not seen before.

What was the Great Commission to the early church? It surely was not to get comfortable in a man-made religious lifestyle or go to church on Sunday and call that salvation. It was a bold sending and commissioning to go into dark places, push back the darkness, and bring light to those who were sick or wounded by the enemy. Of course, the church is a place where we meet and worship the Lord. But the real work of the gospel extends far beyond the walls of a building. It is a bold movement of people willing to fight the good fight of faith and fearlessly take on the work of the devil in the mighty name of Jesus. It is to take back territory in the lives of others that have been oppressed and lead them to the One who came to set them free.

CHAPTER ELEVEN

Prophecy and Fulfillment

The vision that God had given me so many years ago in that prison cell was now coming to pass. I am in awe of how every intricate detail came together. Between the vision, the circumstances making the land available, the logistic and economic complexity of pulling together resources and labor, God had His Spirit and Hand in every detail of it down to the last drawing and the last legal document.

This was not the invention of any man, but the creation of a Holy Spirit-led movement that broke down barriers and established unity in the Spirit for a great work of healing and deliverance. This had God's distinct signature on it. The complexities were far too vast for it to be the work of any one human being's plan or agenda. Its intentions were not to make money, nor to grow a man-made movement. It was made manifest out of the very thoughts and intentions of the heart of Jesus to seek and save that which was lost, to restore the sanctity of human life, and to bring healing to a society that was reeling from the enemy's devastation.

The stage was set. The Master had put His plan in motion. The capital campaign, "Captivity to Destiny" had raised close to $850,000.00 which included finances, donated materials and labor. We had finally come to the place where the land development plan was approved and the lots were all brought under one deed. We got the go ahead from the township for the water and sewer plan and the locations for all the buildings. The drawings were ready, and the architect had completed the blueprints for two group homes, an on-site directors house, and a pavilion.

In order to begin implementation, four existing cabins had to be demolished. Forty-nine trees had to be removed to make space for this new facility. I watched thirty years of family memories being torn down and a beautiful, wooded lot becoming what felt like a war zone for a period of time. Dumpster after dumpster were filled by a huge track-hoe and the cabin debris was hauled away. There was a tearing down and rebuilding of my soul during this process. Every memory, good and bad, was visited as tree after tree, building after building, came down. I was under construction in my spirit as the property was being totally destroyed and raised up to new life. My oneness with this undertaking could hardly be put into words. With every tree that fell there was a sorrow and a hope that was being reborn. Isaiah 61:4 says, "And they shall rebuild the ancient ruins; they shall raise up the former desolations and renew the ruined cities, the devastations of many generations."

I was living in this Scripture. It was as much a part of the work of God as it had become a part of me. I was seeing things through His eyes and not just my own. His will for my life and my will for my life were coming into perfect alignment. It became clear that in all the years of loss, pain, sorrow, grief and confusion, I was being prepared for a time such as this. It was all part of a divine plan. His goodness and mercy overwhelmed me.

I was truly a raptured heart. The only thing that mattered to me was to chase God with my whole heart and tell the world of His goodness and mercy and grace. As David was a man after God's own heart, so would I become. This was the most sacred of assignments that I was ever given the privilege to be a part of. My entire life had been about the unfolding of this marvelous plan and this movement of His Spirit.

There were times during this process that I felt like Jesus was actually standing there with us. I could sense His smile, and His goodness filled my heart. It was as real to me as sitting with a loving father can be. He would look at me and tell me that He was proud of me and that I was doing His will. How I longed for those words all my life from my earthly father. I now abide in my Heavenly Father's loving presence every single day of my life!

After the demolition phase, we began to dig the foundations for the first two houses. This was a unique situation in itself, as the excavators were the father and brother of a former student of The Potter's House. The young man had left the program and several years later had fallen back into his addictive lifestyle and died as the result of an overdose. These men had a heart to help establish a safe place of refuge for the lost and addicted and were helping to fuel the vision. We became such good friends during this project and they were able to come back later and shared their story with the current students.

Lloyd Hoover, Executive Director of The Potter's House, and I had designed the houses to meet the needs of the program as God showed us. An architect from the plain community had stepped up and volunteered to do the blueprints for the houses. I delivered the plans to the township for approval in April 2019. The building inspector came out and approved the site and in July of 2019 we broke ground for this new facility.

The Board of Directors of The Potter's House Ministry continued to give time and finances and were invested in this work. Their faithful prayers and amazing ability to trust the Lord in matters that looked impossible to men continued to move the project forward.

One day I was walking the site and I heard a voice in my spirit saying, "This house will be built upon the Word of God." I paused and waited for God to reveal what this meant. He said that I should create in the natural everything that should play out in the spiritual. So that is what I did. When they went to pour the footers for the basement walls, we wrote scriptures and placed them in the concrete. One of those scriptures was 1 Corinthians 3:11: "For no one can lay any foundation other than the one we already have, Jesus Christ." We placed scripture in every foundation wall of the basement, every wall and every room including the entry door pads. They read, "Behold, I stand at the door and knock; if anyone hears My voice and opens the door, I will come in and eat with that person, and they with Me" (Revelation 3:20).

All the teaching rooms were given a theme that is scripturally suited for what the Lord would use that specific area to accomplish. The teaching room had Colossians 3:16: "Let the word of Christ richly dwell within you, with all wisdom, teaching and admonishing one another with psalms and hymns and spiritual songs, singing with thankfulness in your hearts to God." That Spirit continues to permeate the atmosphere of each room. Those words are alive and the place is on holy ground. Almost everyone who comes here experiences an open portal to the realm of heaven. We have witnessed many signs, wonders, and miracles, not only in the transformation of the property, but more importantly in the hearts and lives of those who come.

We experienced the building of community and the outpouring of generosity during the construction. The selfless sacrifice of those who donated labor and materials was staggering. I took every opportunity to make lunch for the men who would come to work in various phases of construction. I would share my testimony of how the Lord brought this vision out of the pits of despair and the fire of adversity. This indeed was a move of God unlike anything I had ever been a part of.

The details were astounding! The design was masterfully laid out in the natural as well as in the spiritual. People who would have otherwise never crossed paths in life were brought into a divine alignment. The Lord had a much larger plan than we could even understand. Alliances were formed as various levels of the community worked together in one accord for a purpose that was greater than any of us. These included government agencies, water and sewer departments, and state and local support from people who held offices in our state government. Local authorities seemed to embrace this project with less red tape than we anticipated.

Lawyers had to work together to hash out the details in the interstate transfer of properties. Land developers were involved. The Department of Natural Resources had to approve how it would affect the foliage and wildlife due to the river running through the property. There were architects and excavators, builders and tradesmen, and custom craftsmen hired to do some of the unique finish carpentry in the cathedral ceilings. Flooring specialists and kitchen cabinet specialists, interior and exterior specialists would craft these beautiful dwellings and create this holy place for the display of the Lord's splendor.

Process upon process seemed to line up in remarkable preordained timing. We rarely had to wait for a contractor or a supplier to deliver and complete his part of the project to be ready for the next phase. It seemed that the Lord was orchestrating every detail. Things came together with very little effort from those of us who were overseeing construction. No one could explain how all these puzzle pieces came together at such an accelerated rate in light of past experiences with delays in other projects such as this.

As we went into the new year in 2020, we were in awe of what we had been a part of and how God had organized and executed this work. There was even a prophetic message regarding the time when the center would be opened. 20/20 represents perfect vision and this vision was perfected in the year 2020.

The capital campaign was launched in September of 2017. Everything was planned and approved, funds had been raised, and the construction began in July 2019. The facility was opened for ministry on March 25th, 2020. Surely there was a divine Architect and Builder orchestrating all this from above. I have witnessed the miraculous and I have seen the impossible bend to will of God. In my honest opinion, this was none other than a miracle of God.

He was preparing a place for the work of Jesus as described in Isaiah. The spirit of Jesus would carry on and prevail in this place. The brokenhearted would be bound up and freedom would be proclaimed in the lives of the captives. This would be a place where the prisoners could be released from darkness and find comfort for their weary souls. We could endow them with beauty instead of ashes and lead them to the oil of joy instead of a spirit of mourning. They could be clothed with the garments of praise instead of a spirit of despair and they could be granted a double portion instead of their shame. They could find rest for their souls and hope for their future. This had all the makings of an Isaiah 61 ministry in a Psalms 23 atmosphere. The Lord had planned it for such a time as this.

We were all experiencing the full weight of glory that God had assigned to this mission. It was so overwhelming at times that I would sit in the middle of everything and break down in tears as I relived all the pain and trials of my life that God had used to birth this ministry. I saw everything in a compellingly different light. The Lord had used the adversity in my life to strengthen me for this time. He had allowed the brokenness so that I could minister healing to the broken and give hope to the hopeless. A passion and a mission were birthed in my heart for transformational ministry through the power of the resurrected Lord Jesus Christ.

I had a burning in my heart to lead other people to the foot of this illuminated cross that I had encountered so many years before in that prison cell. When we receive such a great and glorious salvation we cannot turn back to the elemental forces of evil in this world and expect to live out the overcomer lifestyle that Christ died to give us. There will come a time in every believer's life where they will have to pick up their cross and follow Jesus Christ. No more excuses of not being ready. Jesus gave His very life to bring us out of a sin-stained and broken world and He fully intends to finish the work that He started in us. The same power that brought Jesus out of the grave is the same power that can raise your life out of the pit of despair. This resurrection power is the regenerated life in the Spirit! It is a heart and mind captivated by the love of God and infused with a revelation of His supernatural indwelling Spirit.

After the official opening of our ministry center, the student house was soon at maximum capacity. My wife Beth and I love what God has us doing. We embrace the title of "Mom and Pop" to the many hearts the Lord brings to us for healing. I sold my home remodeling and repair business to the ministry as a cottage business to provide ongoing support for The Potter's House.

I was all in. I had broken the plow of how I forged a living for decades and went from a remodeler of houses to a remodeler of lives. Just as Jesus had told Peter to follow Him and He would make him a "fisher of men," I heard in my spirit to follow Him and He would make me a remodeler of lives. In this divine transferal, I found myself doing in the Spirit what I had done all my life in the natural. But this was so much more gratifying.

The pursuit of financial gain no longer seemed to have a grip on me. I knew that the Lord was going to meet our needs. I could focus on the transformational ministry that had been birthed out of my own experiences. Everyone can live the transformed life that

Christ purchased for us through His death, burial and resurrection. He died so that we could be forgiven but He rose again so that we could be made alive again. Therein lies the power of the resurrected Savior for all who choose to believe and place their faith and hope in Him. The Scriptures explain in I Corinthians 1:1,8 "For the message of the cross is foolishness to those who are perishing, but to us who are being saved it is the power of God unto salvation."

For many years I had heard these things, but it wasn't until I believed them that the power of God was made manifest in my heart and my life. Until I truly believed this, I looked at Jesus as my Savior but did not experience the power of the resurrection. The resurrected life comes directly from Him conquering death, hell, and the grave on our behalf and granting us this power through His resurrection and ascension. We died with Him, and in baptism we are raised with Him as we surrender our lives and subject ourselves to the resurrected power of the risen Savior.

This is my testimony. God has called me to lead other lost souls to the same Lord who saved me. "While we were yet sinners, Christ died for us" (Romans 5:8). We didn't have to have our "act" together; we didn't have to study for this certificate of being born again. We didn't have to work our way into our salvation and surely, we didn't deserve this great gift. But He loved us and offers us redemption and newness of life. We overcome by the blood of the Lamb and the word of our testimony—not through our own merit, intelligence, looks, or social status. It doesn't matter if you come from jail or if you come from Yale, He is an equal opportunity Savior.

From start to finish this was truly a work of God. In three years, The Potter's House Ministry had doubled its capacity for students including a women's program called The Potter's House of Ruth.

For the twenty years prior, they had dealt strictly with men. God was responding amid the vicious attack of the enemy. The opioid epidemic is a scourge on our entire country. He was creating space for His redemptive power to rescue lives of those caught in addition.

What an amazing story of God's grace! He redeemed me, gifted me, and allowed my story to become part of His story! I am forever grateful for all that He has done and will continue to do through me and through His work at the Potter's House at Still Water's Recovery Center. If you do not know this amazing God and what He can do for you, I invite you to read on and find your place in becoming *A Raptured Heart*

CHAPTER TWELVE

Healing and Deliverance

Every human being on the planet has been wounded by the traumas of life to one degree or another: death of a parent or sibling, abandonment or rejection by a loved one, loss of a relationship that we thought was going to last a lifetime. Maybe we were passed over for the promotion that we thought that we deserved. Maybe we were not picked for the lead in a school play, or we weren't chosen for the position on the high school football team we desperately wanted. These events accumulate over the years and attach themselves to our hearts. They can feel like a weight of bricks that God never intended for us to carry. Disappointments are a part of life and not one person alive is exempt from them. There is no such thing as a pain-free life this side of heaven. The question is, how do we navigate the wide range of emotional challenges we face each and every day of our lives?

"I'm glad you asked." This is where your journey out of bondage to self begins. Before we are born again, we live in our flesh and react to the world and our circumstances on the basis of how we feel. We think it is normal. Yes, God gave us feelings, so they are not bad. They are, in fact, good. But how we choose to use those feelings may be the underlying issue in how we perceive ourselves and the world that we live in. What if our circumstances did not have the power to dictate how we feel, and what if our perception of our circumstances could change that whole dynamic? Then we would have the power to take those thoughts captive before they take us hostage and lead us into a hurtful place in our mind and emotions.

What if there were a way to think and process life so that no human being, circumstance, or situation had the power to "ruin your day"? What if your circumstances or situations are not the issue? What if your perception of your circumstances and situations is the issue? Did you ever realize that you were focusing on a problem that seemed to have no solution? Excellent! Now you may be willing to listen to an entirely different way of looking at these things that seem to be overwhelming to you.

What would it be like to be overwhelmed by God's love for you instead of the problems and challenges you are facing? What if His strength could become your strength? Philippians 4:13 states, "I can do all things through Christ Who gives me strength." Do you believe that? I mean, really believe that? Or are you just familiar with the verse? Have you made it your own in the way you look at life and approach all the challenges that you face? It is one thing to read the Scriptures, but it is a different thing to apply the Scriptures in the way you process life. Many people know about God without really knowing God. They read His Word and say that they believe in Jesus, but when the issues of life come at them, they lose the ability to apply God's Word to their own circumstances.

Without this relationship we face things out of brokenness and our learned patterns for processing the trials of life. We can make a mess of things. God's love for us is so overwhelmingly life altering. When we realize the full extent to which He went to redeem us and save us, we never look at life the same way again.

God our Father sent Jesus to restore the relationship between God and man and to give us the power of a resurrected life. He did this so that we could grasp the fact that He came to destroy the works of the devil and end our captivity in sin. By raising Jesus back to life, He displayed His sovereignty over death and life and demonstrated that all power comes directly through Him into the lives of those He loves. Jesus really did cancel your debt to the law and through God's grace entirely changed the covenant between God and man forever. Jesus didn't just die for you, He died as you! He died for all of your negative emotions, cynicism, and sarcasm. He died so that you could be forgiven but rose again so that your way of life and your way of thinking could undergo a resurrection as well!

It is wonderful that we accept Jesus as Savior at the time of salvation. But what about the twenty, thirty, or even forty years in which you have learned destructive patterns of processing life and behaviors based on thoughts and feelings? The patterns we had adopted have to undergo a transformation as well. These patterns are referred to in Scriptures as "strongholds" in our minds. They can rule and dictate our attitudes and behaviors and destroy our ability to experience peace and joy regardless of our circumstances.

When we process life with Christ, this invitation is incredibly freeing and boldly empowering. He really is intimately in love with man and wants to set us free from the destructive patterns of this world as well as the generational and ungodly belief systems that have been set up through our life's experiences and learned behaviors. This is not a new set of rules or traditions that we must conform to in order to be accepted by God. It is an invitation to live a new and resurrected life free from the bondage of the past and harmful, destructive patterns of thinking. When Jesus ascended back to the Father, He promised to send us an Advocate, the Holy Spirit. He said that the Holy Spirit would be our Counselor.

The Holy Spirit enables us to move between the realm of heaven and earth and be heard on high through Jesus Christ who sits at the right hand of the Father contantly making intercession for us. Ephesians 2:6 states, "For He has raised us up with Christ and seated us with Him in the heavenly realms in Christ Jesus." Salvation is not a work of man, but is totally dependent on a God of great love. You see, our salvation is not something that we can earn or deserve. We can only believe it in order to be qualified to receive it.

So how do we approach this process of renewing our minds and being made right in the sight of God through Christ? First, we have to humble ourselves and admit to God that we have messed up our own lives and we desperately need His help. Then we have to accept that God has made a provision for our failures in that He gave His one and only Son to offer Himself as an atoning sacrifice for our sins and to restore us back to a right relationship with Him. He loves us and wants to wash away our sins and make us clean so that we can walk in a way that is pleasing to Him. Once we have believed on the Lord Jesus Christ for our salvation, we have been qualified for the sanctifying and cleansing work of God in our messed-up lives.

So, what part does the Holy Spirit play in this process? First of all, He carries the affairs of our lives to the throne room of God where Jesus sits and intercedes for us. We need to confess the sins that we carry around and the guilt and shame of all we have done that would keep us in bondage and unable to approach God. Then we ask the Holy Spirit to advocate for us and renounce the learned patterns of behavior that come from our fallen way of approaching our relationship to a Holy God.

Ah, the power of forgiveness! Forgiveness is the key that unlocks the door to the transformation that we are all seeking. Do you realize that unforgiveness is poison to the human soul? Resentment is like drinking the poison that you want someone who offended you to die from! All human conflict is birthed out of unforgiveness. If left unresolved, it will spread like cancer throughout the entirety of a person's life and take them captive to a root of bitterness. This can manifest itself in a thousand different forms of malignancy in attitudes and even in the physical condition of the individual trapped in unforgiveness.

When a person is hurt or abused by a parent, the devil uses unforgiveness to hold them hostage and destroy the sanctity of family. The trust relationship that God designed for parents to have with their children and children with their parents is dismantled and the enemy takes over. If these wounds are left unhealed, the pain will perpetuate for generations and the mistrust and dysfunction of family will become the norm. The end result of this is known as a generational curse. Alcoholism, drug addiction, and many other things can be transmitted from generation to generation. There is a God-sized hole in each person's soul. We end up seeking for ways to fill the voids where those needs are not properly satisfied.

Those who struggle with addiction did not set out with the goal of becoming a drug addict or an alcoholic. I am absolutely sure they will tell you that this was not their intention. They are just trying to fill a void or trying to drown out painful memories of abandonment or abuse. All kinds of underlying forces drive their behavior. They are acting out of pain either consciously or unconsciously. These abuses or wounds, left unhealed, become the forces that drive and destroy lives, relationships and families. I have come to the conclusion that addiction is not the problem that our society battles with; it is brokenness and unresolved pain. Wounded people who seem to gravitate toward other wounded people and practice drunkenness and drug addiction are trying to fill the voids of feeling unloved and unaccepted.

I really don't understand the dynamics of a society that wants to build more prisons for the wounded people who act out than to build healing centers that can help bring healing to wounded hearts. You can't punish a person into right behavior; they have been punished enough! That is what is driving the behavior. On the other hand, you can love a person into right behavior and teach them to forgive and heal their past so that they can be restored to a right relationship with God and man. This is the passion that drives me. It is the heart of how I minister.

Some of these wounds are deep and very painful for individuals to talk about. I have been in settings where the Holy Spirit used a song to bring a person to a flood of tears and emotions that had been left unhealed for decades. Once the wounds are revealed, they can begin to be healed. At times, the words of a song pierce an individual's heart and God ministers deeply through the message contained in the music.

I do a group called Empower Hour. The name indicates the impact of Christ on the wounded heart. Jesus exemplified forgiveness in a way that most human beings view as impossible. I have walked with so many broken people who say that they have been praying for years for God to take away a burden, when He has actually been asking them to just release it to Him all that time. Too many people go to God and ask Him to take away extreme pain, yet they hold on to it like a morbid friend. Let go! God isn't going to heal you by force; that is not how He works. We need to surrender those pains and wounds to Him for healing. Only then can the Holy Spirit begin to restore wholeness with God and others.

What if we learned to pray with God as much as we pray out of desperation to God? Jesus sits at the right hand of the Father to make intercession for us. It has been and always will be God's desire that none should perish but that we all come to Him for healing and restoration. He is never going to change His mind about that. God loves us so much that He even gave us the means through which we can be restored and healed. Have you ever thought about coming into agreement with God for your own healing? Why are you holding on to pain that can only delay your healing and the restoration of God's intended purposes for your life? Does what I am saying resonate with you? Have you ever found healing in holding a grudge or refusing to forgive someone?

I love what Isaiah shares in Isaiah 55: 8-9: "For my thoughts are not your thoughts, neither are your ways my ways, declares the Lord. As the heavens are higher than the earth, so are my ways higher than your ways and My thoughts higher than your thoughts." He lives in a place of perfection where there is no sin or brokenness, and He invites us to live with Him in that place as well. Once you accept Jesus as your Savior, you are adopted as one of God's own children. God is in great favor of healing His children and restoring them to wholeness. If we give ourselves to this process, we enter training to become a new creation in a right relationship with God.

What do you have to lose but all the things that would bind and hold you captive to a worldly and carnal perception of your life? God wants to rewrite your story! Are you going to allow Him to do so, or are you going to hold on to those things that are keeping you stuck? Do you want to give a part of your life to Christ and hold back areas that you feel you can't trust Him with? He can't heal something that you are unwilling to surrender. He wants us to deeply desire Him and His salvation so He can heal us. Without forgiveness there is no true healing, and without Jesus we can never truly experience God's redemption and salvation at the level at which God intends.

The way we were brought up leaves a profound impression on the way we will process life as we learn and grow in our relationships with others. If our parents had a broken past, we will have learned to process life through the brokenness that was handed down to us. These inherited models can set up a dynamic in our minds and hearts known as ungodly belief systems. There is a vast contrast between what we learned growing up and what God intended for us to learn.

If you were raised in a God-fearing family, your chances of understanding the ways and the things of God have a larger capacity to influence the way you think and process life. On the other hand, a person who had parents who were not in a relationship with God through Jesus, learned mostly a worldly system of processing life.

Even if a person is brought up going to church, there is no guarantee that they learned a relationship with God as a lifestyle. They may have learned traditional church doctrines but still fall short of the love relationship that God intends to have with all believers. In this case, one may end up worshipping church doctrines at the expense of a vibrant living relationship with the One who gives life.

In either case, we have the potential to miss the very heart of what God wants to accomplish in our lives for eternity. Trading the knowledge of God for what your parents taught you or trading the freedom that salvation brings for religious tradition would be missing the whole point of why Jesus died. We must be very careful to not adopt the doctrines of men or religion and mistake them for the way to salvation. While the church is God's institution established here on earth to carry out His work, Jesus—not someone who founded a religion—is the Head of the church. We should remain mindful of how we represent the kingdom of God to the lost and how we invite them into this great salvation.

Jesus is the one and only true Way to God and eternal life. In our own efforts, we will always fall short of the glory of God. Many wars have been fought over religious beliefs. Since the beginning of time as we know it, religion has caused more wars than the fights for wealth and territory combined. Proverbs 14:12 states, "There is a way that seems right to a man, but its end leads to death." This can mean the death of tens of thousands of people or the death of an entire nation or dynasty. The stories of the rise and fall of many great kings and kingdoms is recorded in the Bible for us to learn from so that we may take a different pathway. "The written law brings death, but the Spirit brings life and peace." (See 2 Corinthians 3:6; Romans 8:6)

After uncovering the wounds in an individual's heart, it is imperative that we facilitate an atmosphere where the Holy Spirit and the individual can enter a place of agreement. Then the work of the Spirit and the process of confessing and renouncing these newly discovered broken and dysfunctional areas of the person's life can begin to be healed. The Holy Spirit wishes to replace the lies that have been planted by the enemy with sound biblical truths about the person's identity. Once those strongholds are removed, they can be replaced with thoughts tinctured with the fruit of the Spirit as the new approach to life.

I have walked with people who have been in and out of secular psychological and clinical rehabilitation programs. The distinct difference between these and faith-based programs is that they offer conflict resolution or behavior modification while faith-based programs offer life altering transformation in the very perception of what life means. Having had decades of experience with both approaches, I maintain that the faith dynamic is undoubtedly more lasting and impactful. When people ask me for statistics, I offer this answer: "Faith-based transformation works one hundred percent of the time for those who are committed to staying on the healing journey. God's love never fails. I can't tell you what other programs can do, but I can tell you what the power of God can do. It brings resurrection power into the life of spiritually dead people. They can be made alive again and go on to do great things in the kingdom of God and in the lives of others."

Deliverance, according to Webster's Dictionary, is "the act of delivering someone or something: especially liberation, rescue; an opinion or decision such as a verdict of a jury expressed publicly." This clearly applies to the finished work of Christ on the cross and what Jesus accomplished for us. Our sins were judged on the cross. We were also judged on the cross; we were judged "worthy of God's love." Just before Jesus breathed His last breath and gave up His Spirit on the cross, He said the words "It is finished." What was finished? What did He mean? The debt we owed God for our sins was paid in full! He took our punishment upon Himself so that we would not have to stand in the judgment of God's wrath for our sins. He delivered us from sin and death into the glorious love and perfect grace of God for our redemption! It was a supreme act of agape love that was displayed to deliver the entire world back to a posture of right standing with God.

This is marvelous in our sight and life altering for those who get it, I mean, who really get it! For men and women who realize the extent to which God went to redeem their lives and deliver them back into His kingdom, His love is divine deliverance and all-encompassing. But Jesus didn't stop there. He went down into the grave, descended into hell, and took the keys of death, hell and the grave from the devil. He triumphantly resurrected from the dead to model our way to deliverance. He overcame death on our behalf so that we could be delivered into a resurrected life of service to Him and into a promise of eternal life with Him in the hereafter.

When I contemplate the word deliverance, it comes to mind that in order to go be delivered, a person or a package has to be released from a place of holding such as a warehouse or a place of captivity. As sinful human beings we are all held captive in sin from the day we are born. Romans 5:12 states, "Therefore, just as sin came into the world through one man (Adam), and death through sin, and so death spread to all men because all sinned." This is a condition that we are all born into. None of us asked to be born into a world in this condition, but we cannot change it. In that state, we are also predestined to find our way to Jesus so that we can be born a second time. Being born from above, reborn of the Spirit of God, is what it means to be 'born again."

We literally are born twice in our lifetime. When we accept Christ as our Savior, we are delivered just like the day we came out of our mother's womb in a natural delivery. Once we were born of natural birth and by the will of man. In the second birth, we are reborn from above and adopted as one of God's children to become a joint heir with Jesus to the kingdom of heaven. We were once children of the flesh but when we are born again, we become children of God. As newborn children, we learn to walk in the attributes of our heavenly Father and learn how to be a child of the King. A kingdom child acts differently than a natural one because we have been delivered into the kingdom of our Father's love. When we realize this adoption has occurred, we become eager to learn the ways and the benefits of being a child of God. We desire to know the full weight of glory and responsibility that it carries.

We all need to be delivered out of our old nature and into our new nature. We are delivered from one realm of being into a whole other realm of being and begin to manifest the attributes of a child who is born of God. We receive a new inheritance, not one that lasts only as long as we live, but an eternal inheritance that will go on for eternity with God in His kingdom. How precious is the adoption of a child of God! How wonderful are the benefits of knowing the Savior who delivered us into this great and marvelous salvation!

I am not talking about merely enhancing a person's financial status. That would tremendously undervalue the gift that we receive as adopted children of the living God. When we become God's child, we receive His attributes as well. We inherit the fruits of the Spirit as the character defining our new man. Love, joy, peace, patience, kindness, goodness, gentleness and self-control are all part of our spiritual inheritance and the character in which we abide. These are just a few of the many blessings we inherit as children of the King. We also learn to walk with purpose. We deal with others with integrity. We live in a posture of giving to the world instead of getting from the world. Our lives and the desires of our hearts undergo a major re-alignment.

The things that God sees as important and valuable to His children are the very same things that we adopt as important and valuable in our own lives. His will for our lives becomes our will for our lives as we hunger and thirst for goodness and righteousness. We no longer accept the foolish patterns of the world defining right and wrong, good and evil, permissible or not permissible. Let's talk of cigarette smoking, for example. The world and society say it is legal. But when I come into the kingdom, I understand that my body is the temple of the Holy Spirit and cigarettes are harmful to that temple. Why would I harm my temple? The world glorifies success as more money, a bigger house, nicer cars, luxurious boats, and excess in every area of life. But the Lord Himself said in Matthew 6:31, "So do not worry, saying, 'What shall we eat?' or 'What shall we drink?' or 'What shall we wear?' For the pagans run after these things, and your heavenly Father knows that you need them."

If we spend forty to fifty hours a week pursuing financial gain or taking care of our possessions, but only spend an hour a week seeking God in the Scriptures and an hour a week in church, what does that say about our priorities? Matthew 6:21 says, "For where your treasure is, there your heart will be also." This should indeed challenge us to examine what we truly value and what we say we value.

If we profess to be born-again yet all evidence shows a pursuit of financial gain and a possession-focused life, then we are lying to ourselves. Remember this, money is not the root of all evil. It is the love of money and the worship of money that is evil. When we put our wealth and social status above our commitment and our relationship with God, we are not aligning ourselves with the purposes of God. He loves His children with a passion beyond the love of this world and He also provides for them with an extravagant love. We are called to love and have hearts of hospitality and generosity that only can be found in the ongoing, abiding love of God. He is the giver of all good gifts and the One who judges the motives of all that we do.

We need to be delivered out of a worldly system of values and delivered into a kingdom economy and culture. The Word of God says, "He who sows sparingly, will also reap sparingly but he who sows abundantly will also reap abundantly" (2 Corinthians 9:6). These kingdom principles cannot be violated. The Word further declares: "The Lord gives, and the Lord takes away" (Job 1:21). "Pride comes before the fall" (Proverbs 16:18). Look at a man who is full of his own selfish ambitions, and I will show you a lonely man. Your bank account and your investments cannot keep you warm at night or care for you when you are sick. If a man squanders his wealth and loves money more than his children or wife, he will surely lose them.

The opposite of greed is a poverty spirit: always seeking and never finding, always hoping but never obtaining. A poverty spirit is not about a lack of financial resources. It is about a dearth in a person's character and the inability to manifest creativity. The poverty spirit always thinks the worst without considering the best. It gives a downtrodden perception of self that limits one's ability to rise to any occasion or step up and seize opportunities. Proverbs

29:18 says, "Where there is no vision the people perish." Many individuals seem to always be in need yet do not apply scriptural knowledge in a way that could lift them out of that need.

God wants our lives to be purpose driven. He wants to fuel us with ambition and direction. Without His vision for our lives, we can become stagnant and ineffective in all our aspirations. If you don't have a vision, then find someone who does. Partner with them until God uses them to inspire vision in you. Vision and passion are contagious; God loves a passionately driven soul. Look at King David. He was known as a man after God's own heart. When you read the Psalms, the man's passion just oozes off the pages. He bore his heart before God and fervently repented of his sins and shortcomings!

Was David a perfect man? Absolutely not. But he was a passionate man. He made some huge blunders that wrought consequences into his life. He broke covenant with God on many levels. But if you want to practice repentance, David is a great model. Do you think that David is in heaven after committing adultery and having one of his mighty men, Uriah killed in battle so that He could hide his sin with Bathsheba? The Old Testament law would say that a man like David was beyond redemption. But God loved him in spite of his flaws and failures. David still forged God's kingdom here on earth and took Jerusalem for the Lord. His son Solomon built the temple of God and established a culture of the kingdom in his day.

Solomon was worse than his father when it came to lust issues. He had three hundred wives and nine hundred concubines. His eyes were never satisfied. Do you think that these men are in heaven? With all that sin, a legalist would say surely not! But God called David a man after His own heart and charged Solomon to build His temple.

Indeed, God's ways are not man's ways and what God thinks is higher than what man thinks. I have studied those who had uniquely close relationships with God such as many of the Old Testament prophets. A similarity runs true with almost all of them: they were flawed. They were not the pedigree that man would call qualified for the roles that they played, yet they shaped the world and our moral laws for centuries. Moral laws and ethical standards were given to entire nations through the relationships that these men had with the Father of all creation.

Even the United States Constitution was written out of the hearts and minds of men of God that carried these moral laws in their hearts and refused to bow the knee to tyranny. The human spirit to overcome incredible odds and to dare to dream is at the very foundation of what made America a free nation. These men were willing to fight for the chance to live as free men and have their own lands and their own homes filled with sanctity and safety under the watchful eye of God. Men of vision and passion forged the very fabric of our social systems and made us one of the greatest nations on the face of the earth. But what happens when we begin to turn from those values and put prosperity above God? What happens when we abandon God in our schools, calling good evil and compromising our moral and ethical freedoms?

Deliverance! This is what we need as individuals and what we need as a nation. Deliverance involves returning to the biblical values that we were founded upon, and reviving things of God which made us a great nation. This deliverance will rekindle a passion for God-centered pursuits and restore run-down areas of our towns. It is deliverance into a kingdom mindset and unity in the spirit of the people of God to accomplish great and mighty things. It will lead all members of society to work together outside of a competitive spirit. When His will is being done on earth as it is in heaven—when His bride is ready—Jesus will indeed return.

What would deliverance into a God-centered vision do for our society? For one, the quality of living would be better for everyone. Families would be healed by working together for the common good. Everyone would have enough because people would willingly give of their resources and their talents to create God's goodness as a lifestyle. The Spirit of the Living God would abide in the hearts and minds of men and women and our children would no longer be victims of broken families.

If we were delivered into God's intentions for us, there would be no more trying to outdo each other for the next big promotion. Instead, we would be honoring one another above ourselves. We would have hearts to reach back and pull our brother or sister forward. Our resources would be used for more than our own selfish ambitions. It would be a "we" centered society instead of a "me" centered society.

Prisons would start to close with healing as the new normal. People would know that they are loved and that they belong to a purpose greater than themselves. With God at the center of our society, being His child, part of His kingdom, would be more than enough. You may call me a dreamer, but that's what they called me when I shared the vision for the Still Waters Recovery Center campus of The Potter's House Ministry. Now, we are making a difference in the lives of those who come. We are setting a community on fire for revival and the things of God.

The faith community, recovery community and the business community all came together, and local government officials backed us. People of all trades came together to create a sacred place for the lost and broken. I witnessed the kingdom of God working together on a level that I have never seen before or have been privileged to be a part of in my lifetime. The vision was God's, the plan was God's, and the divine connections were God's. This place will continue to carry the anointing of what it was created for long after those who God used to create it are gone. His purposes to redeem the lost will always be at the forefront of deliverance in God's heart.

I will never again believe that anything is impossible if it is according to God's will and in alignment with His purposes. Can you feel the expectation of glory attached to a move of God? Can you catch a God-sized vision for your life, your church, and your community? Can you allow the Holy Spirit to breathe life into that vision?

Miracles happen when we are in one accord with God. We need to become the scriptures—not just read them or know them. We are called to have the Word of God dwell in us richly so that we can demonstrate His power and glory here on earth. Those to whom God has called us will be set free to live a delivered and resurrected life. Oh, how glorious is it to partake in the divine nature of the God who saves, the God who redeems and the God who restores.

Matthew 10:8 commissions us, "Freely you have received; freely give; Heal the sick, raise the dead, cleanse those with leprosy and drive out demons." Deliverance is about accepting and fulfilling the commission to do what Jesus commissioned us to do. If we are truly His disciples, then these things should be our normal mode of operation. His manifest authority transferred to those who belong to Him gives us the same authority here on earth as Jesus had. It is miraculous that Jesus did these things, not as a divine being but as a man fully yielded to God.

Delivering people from the bondage of demonic oppression is what we have been called to do. Do you realize that people who are caught up in addictions are also caught up in witchcraft? It might sound radical or crazy to people who think from a worldly point of view, but in Greek the word for "sorcery" is pharmakeia from which we derive the word pharmacy in the English language. It can also mean magic, witchcraft, enchantment, drugs or medication. All of these demonic practices oppress people's feelings and emotions and destroy people's lives. It is very real! The astronomical death toll of the opioid crisis demonstrates it. In the year 2020 there were 92,000 confirmed drug overdose deaths across this country. Many started with a doctor's prescription for pain killers which led to a heroin addiction. A deceived society tries to justify this as "choice." But it is much more. It is a spiritual battle between the forces of evil and the power of the Living God.

As a society we need to stop buying into every newfound remedy that is available and learn to walk a life of sound discretion. The enemy always over-promises and underdelivers through telling us only a portion of the truth. That is why he is called the "father of lies." He only comes to steal, kill and destroy everything that is good and holy. He hates God and His children with a malignancy that is vile. We need godly wisdom to understand his tactics so that we do not fall into his snare.

There is more going on in our lives and our relationship with God than what we can understand until we are delivered from the strongholds in our minds. These strongholds create thought patterns that will play out and manifest themselves in ways that God had never intended. We will react out of past negative experiences and look at life from the viewpoint of a victim. Overcoming this mindset requires much more than psychological therapy; we need the supernatural power of the Holy Spirit to remove those destructive forces and thought patterns. I refer to this process as "divine-transferal."

When our thoughts and emotions begin to come under the control of the Holy Spirit and we align ourselves with our identity instead of our emotions, we are able to experience true freedom. We begin to look at the world through a totally different lens, through the eyes of being "more than a conqueror" rather than a victim. We see the possibilities instead of the problems. We walk in victory rather than victimization. We are delivered into a realm in which we process life through the mind of Christ instead of through our fears and anxieties.

Fear is displaced by faith. Despair is displaced by hope. Unforgiveness is displaced by forgiveness. Joy is birthed out of circumstances that used to hold us hostage to a spirit of heaviness. As love begins to reign and rule in our hearts and minds, we abide under the wings of the Almighty and dwell in the safety of His love and comfort.

We then see life from a compellingly elevated position of authority in the Spirit. We begin to live the scripture that says, "Trust the Lord with all your heart and lean not to your own understanding, in all your ways acknowledge Him and He will direct your paths" (Proverbs 3:5-6). We realize that we have begun to move to the cadence of the heavenly realms as earthbound logic and reason fade in light of this newfound freedom. We are no longer merely reading the Scriptures, but in some supernatural way we have become a living embodiment of them. Confidence and courage are birthed out of what used to be a mindset of defeat. Everything makes perfect sense.

Once healing and deliverance are accomplished through the work of the Holy Spirit and the redemptive power of the cross, we enter a realm of freedom through this act of divine transferal, called, "Identity." The Lord gives us resurrection power in our hearts and minds to live an ascended life, and our identity begins to emerge. This is adoption. The Holy Spirit will teach us to think with a renewed mind, the mind of Christ. As we internalize the promises of God, our entire life moves out of a broken world and adopted into a kingdom mindset. We begin to trade on the promises of God because they are the spiritual currency of heaven—the inheritance we receive through the adoption into God's family. We literally become a new creation in Christ Jesus. The old nature passes away and the character of Christ begins to be formed in us.

No psychological training or behavior modification process can compare to the power of the resurrected life. This is a transformation of the heart and mind that go deeply into the core of who we are as children of the living God. The realization of this new identity manifests in the way we think and respond to every area of life. We approach every trial from a place of victory instead of a victim mindset. We see ourselves as more than conquerors in Christ. "Give thanks to the Lord for he is good. His love endures forever" (Psalm 136:1).

CHAPTER THIRTEEN

Identity and Empowerment

Each one of us has been born into a specific time in history and a specific geographical location. We also are born into a specific family with inherited family dynamics as well as a socio-economic status. The vast variety of people's personalities are molded and formed from immersion in these inherited circumstances. Out of these many facets in the predetermined variations of an individual's background is forged their character through which they interpret life.

We were all born into a sinful and broken world. We have very little or no say in the dynamics that shape and mold us as we grow up. These circumstances are not chosen but are inherited through our earthly families and are passed down from generation to generation.

Some people are fortunate enough to be born into families with a sound faith background. Some are born into lives of privilege and social status. Others are born into families that are impoverished and learn to survive in ways that have nothing to do with good sound moral and ethical lifestyles and behaviors. They are simply not healthy and productive ways of living.

Some are born into wealth and status and do not understand what it means to struggle. They have the best of education and live prosperous lives—but are driven by the desire to be successful. They do not have a biblical view of wealth and success and do not know how to steward what they have been given. Their way of life is self-made. Don't misunderstand this. God is the Father of all blessings and men are not actually self-made. However, there is an illusion of self-reliance. Life is lived out of human effort rather than dependence on God. Many different worldly influences and attributes go into shaping and molding our character. We all have the free will to choose the paths that we want to follow.

Some people feel trapped in an environment and have surrendered themselves to the lie that there is no way out. Others perceive that life will always be a journey of success and prosperity. They believe that nothing will ever go wrong and those who have helped them achieve success will be there the rest of their lives. When their reason for living is taken away, they fall apart because they have placed all their faith and trust in worldly things. Our identity can either set us up for success or failure. It can dictate the trajectory of our entire lives.

Our perception of who we are sets the stage for all present and future aspirations. What we convey to the rest of the world we live in will manifest in our present and future reality as we grow into what we perceive to be our identity. A human being must see him or herself as prosperous in order to prosper; it doesn't just happen by osmosis and can't be maintained by merely receiving an inheritance and hoping for the best.

If we take a posture of defeatism, we will always come to a place of defeat. If we choose a victim mentality, we will believe that everyone has done us wrong in one way or another. Genuine relationships are impossible because some people will always think that the world owes them retribution for the lack of whatever they didn't get from their family or social background. This identity becomes a destructive force in their lives and the lives of everyone they are in relationship with. These individuals always need to be rescued from their own bad choices and can't seem to take responsibility for their part in causing their own demise. There is always something wrong with everyone else and never anything wrong with them. They hold the world hostage for their failures and cannot own any of their bad choices as the possible cause of their struggles.

Blame-shifting, justification, minimization and rationalization are all hallmark traits through which these individuals process their lives. This sounds crazy to a sane and rational person, but it is reality for countless numbers of broken people in this world due to the faulty belief systems that were developed in the character-building years of their lives.

Perhaps a parent abandoned them or was abusive, a role model let them down or hurt them deeply. Or maybe a loved one passed away that they were entirely too dependent on, and they felt lost without that person in their life. Perhaps they were raised in a drug culture or in a violent neighborhood and learned survival of the fittest. Maybe they went through a devastating divorce.

There are as many reasons for the brokenness as there are individuals. Without a total renewal of identity and thought processes, they will go on to the bitter end, feeling trapped in all of this negativity, never realizing there is a way out. These destructive thought patterns are referred to in the Bible as "strongholds."

In recovery ministry, we have come to know this malady as defects of character or in deliverance ministry as demonic oppression. Most of these have been established through ungodly belief systems passed on from previous generations who believed lies that have nothing to do with biblical, moral or ethical standards for living in a right relationship with God.

This is where identity becomes of paramount importance. Two distinct driving forces are at odds with one another: "Who are we?" and "Where do I fit in this world?" We are born into a human world with human standards, rules and inherited human ways of thinking and acting. That changes the moment we receive Christ and have the opportunity to step into God's kingdom and family in order to receive a new "born again" identity. Our perception and our destination are changed as we are given an eternal trajectory for our lives and the lives of our families.

First, we have to accept Christ as our Savoir and internalize all the benefits that this great love of God offers. A divine transfer of beliefs takes place for those who have chosen to accept Jesus as Lord and not just as Savior. They receive a new identity as a joint heir with Him in the kingdom of heaven and as a born-again child of God.

Galatians 5:19-26 is very clear about what we have been adopted out of and the new identity we have been gifted with. It states, "The acts of the flesh are obvious: sexual immorality, impurity and debauchery; idolatry and witchcraft (drugs); hatred, discord, jealousy, fits of rage, selfish ambition, dissentions, factions and envy; drunkenness, orgies, and the like. I warn you, as I did before, that those who live like this will not inherit the kingdom of God. But the fruit of the spirit is love, joy, peace patience, kindness, goodness, faithfulness, gentleness and self-control. Against such things there is no law. Those who belong to Christ have crucified the flesh with its passions and desires. Since we live by the Spirit, let us keep in step with the Spirit. Let us not become conceited, provoking and envying each other."

Can you see the distinct differences in the characteristics of a man born in the flesh and living in his flesh versus those of a man who has been born again and walks by the Spirit? There is a stark contrast in the value systems by which the two differentiate themselves in their character, thought processes and behavior. Which of the two sounds the most inviting? We can never discover the best in us until we disempower the worst in us and allow the new man character to become our new mode of operation.

"Christ in us is the hope of glory" (Colossians 1:27). "In Him we live and move and have our being" (Acts 17:28). True freedom is the result of a life surrendered to Christ and the empowerment to walk out that life in the Spirit. All other attempts to fill our lives with meaning and purpose will be futile. We will exhaust ourselves in our attempts to fill a God-sized void in our hearts with a man-sized solution. Truth be told, all the human logic and reason that the world has to offer will never make us into who we were created to be in Christ.

The best of us can only begin to emerge when we truly connect with Christ on a heart level and learn to walk out life with Him as Lord. As we spend time in His presence, we will be transformed more and more into His image. The mind of Christ is the most powerful weapon of spiritual warfare that we can possess. It drops the H-bomb on all the enemy's tactics and disempowers the lies of the traditional ways of thinking.

The mind of Christ separates what is true from the Truth that sets men free! It may be true that you were a sinner and that you made some mistakes, but the Truth is that Christ died and rose again to release you from the effects of sin, guilt and condemnation! The same power that raised Jesus from the grave lives in you to raise you up out of the dead works and traditions that have held you captive.

Our part is to believe on Him for our salvation, not our own ability or even our self-punishment. It is by faith and not by works that we are saved. (See Ephesians 2:8-9.) The works are a response to this great salvation, not a way of obtaining it. Romans 3:23 says, "For all have sinned and fallen short of the glory of God." There is nothing we can do or stop doing to qualify us for heaven apart from accepting Christ as the Way, the Truth and the Life.

I don't know about you, but I was ecstatic to receive this salvation and new identity! I didn't want the life I had before Christ. I realized just how empty I was and how futile my attempts to live a good life were.

Salvation and adoption into His kingdom and His family causes us to inherit a divine spiritual DNA that is eternal. The Scriptures say that we have received a deposit; the Holy Spirit is the promise or guarantee of our inheritance for what God promised His people who receive Him. (See Ephesians 1:13-14). Our destiny is secure; our story has been set in motion by our adoption into His family. He begins to write His amazing story of redemption across the pages of our lives as we walk in step with the Spirit, trusting in His plan the whole way home to our heavenly destination.

My deepest heartfelt prayer is that all men would grasp the reality of God's all-consuming and glorious love. The greatness in every man is birthed out of that revelation of God's love poured out and the fierce battle that Jesus fought and won to triumph over death, hell and the grave.

Our truest identity will flow out of that revelation and our submission to His grace, mercy and resurrection power. Without the work of Jesus and the finished work of the cross, all mankind would live a futile life of laws and regulations that would hold us captive to our sins and shortcomings. We would all be held captive to our consciences and live a life of perpetual guilt and condemnation. But Jesus took that all away. (See Colossians 2: 13-15).

Our identity is that of a child of the most high God. It comes with so many benefits they are too numerous to count. He is a good, good Father and our brother happens to be the Savior of the world, Jesus! He is also our Lord, our High Priest and King. There has never been and never will be anyone like Him, the One who redeems and restores us. Jesus is God's final Word to mankind about His love and kind intentions toward us.

The Bible tells us about men in history who did everything they could do to manifest some form of greatness or validity, only to end up on their knees asking God to save them. When we come to the end of ourselves, that is where we find our Savior. Most men have to exhaust all human logic and reason until they come to the true understanding of their deep need for rescue. Jesus is God's rescue plan for all mankind and His character is the model for the redemptive life which we must adopt in order to live in right relationship with a holy God. The deepest desire of our hearts becomes the pursuit of the transformation to His image and character.

2 Corinthians 3:18 states, "And we all, who with unveiled faces contemplate the Lord's glory, are being transformed into His image with ever-increasing glory, which comes from the Lord, who is the Spirit." The manifest presence of the Lord is a trademark characteristic that shines from the heart of every born-again believer who learns the benefits of abiding in the Spirit and taking their prompts from the heavenly throne room of God Himself.

Once again Corinthians 1:18 says, "For the message of the cross is foolishness to those who are perishing, but to us who are being saved it is the power of God unto salvation. For the foolishness of God is wiser than man's wisdom, and the weakness of God is stronger than man's strength." Those who view salvation as foolish can never understand those who have experienced this great resurrection of spirit and have learned to abide in it. Our new identity is the place of power that infuses the life of every believer and enables them to see life through a compellingly different lens.

It is important for every soul to discover this transformational life. Once a soul has tasted and seen how good the Lord is there is birthed an insatiable hunger for more as we explore the vastness of our salvation. The rivers of living waters that Jesus referred to in John 4:1-15 become a constant place of refreshment and deeper hunger. The renewal and regeneration of our minds and hearts is the birthplace for our new identity and these rivers are the source of our wellspring of eternal life. This place of deep abiding is available to every thirsty soul who seeks the Lord.

A lot of people will ask how they can abide in the Lord constantly and still handle responsibilities of career and family. I want to remove all the obstacles of doubt. The abiding lifestyle is developed by including the Lord in your everyday responsibilities and trials as well as triumphs and joys. It is more like developing a constant, personal relational dialogue with the Holy Spirit. It means including Him in all the aspects of your life. Do you include your husband, wife and children in the everyday aspects of your life? Then why is it so difficult to include the Lord in these very same ways? Why is it so difficult to relate to the One who gave us life as a member of our family?

By embracing this reality, you also embrace your new identity. By learning to abide in Him in all the areas of your life, you establish relationship with this loving Father. We learn to be one of His children and part of His family as intended to be since the foundation of the world. Our perfect Father chastens us out of love and guidance and not out of punishment and condemnation. He is not angry with us. On the contrary, He is very much in love with us and yearns for us to reciprocate that love. He gave us free will so that we would not be forced to do anything but can freely choose this walk of love in relationship to Him.

Going to church once a week doesn't establish relationship with God. It may make us more aware of who He is, but it doesn't establish intimate relationship with Him. We can find ourselves mistaking churchianity for true Christianity, which is walking in the abiding love of God as a way of life every single day. Going to church is good and God even tells us not to forsake the gathering of the brethren. But that does not, in itself, qualify us for salvation. Is your life still a series of self-made disciplines and aspirations with you sitting on the throne as you call all the shots and try to control your own destiny?

Getting involved in more ministry, more outreach, and tons of church activities does not qualify us for salvation either. This is works and not relationship. Works will in no way gain you access to heaven when you cross that threshold between here and eternity.

Am I on the throne of my own life? Do I work sixty hours a week, make a lot of money, provide for my family and go to church once a week? Do I spend only five minutes of devotions with the Lord in the morning then not think much about Him the rest of the day? Do I end the day with a ten-second "thank you" for the day's blessings? These habits do not reflect an abiding relationship with God.

This portrayal of an "American Jesus" could be the reasons for many failed marriages and broken families. It manifests in the pursuit of the American Dream rather than the blessings of an abiding relationship with God. On the day that you breathe your last breath, do you want your legacy and your epitaph to read "Here lies a man who worked hard and loved his family. He was involved in many groups of service and served the local church," or do you want it to read, "Here lies a man who had a passionate love for God and for people. He helped to change and transform lives and communities for the glory of God and the advancement of His kingdom"?

Empowerment from above is what we need every day of our lives. Maturity is a hallmark of this born-again identity, and it manifests itself in boldness and authority in the purposes of God for our lives. We are no longer tossed back and forth by our old nature and the things that used to easily ensnare us. We arrive at a place where we can quickly discern truth from lies and good from evil. We know what is from God and what is not from God. We have learned the disciplines of walking in victory. The enemy will be wearied by our steadfast life in the Spirit and realize that he can no longer get an easy win on us. Instead, we become empowered to do battle with him for the hearts and minds of others.

We become warriors in God's army, equipped to tear down every vain imagination that exalts itself against God. We walk filled with the intentions and purposes of our Savior and begin to experience the signs, wonders and miracles that He told the apostles that they would do. Jesus said, "Very truly I tell you, whoever believes in me will do the works I have been doing, and they will do even greater things than these, because I am going to the Father" (John 14:12).

That's right, Jesus told us that we who believe will do even greater things than these because He wanted the life of authority over the enemy to be given to us. He did not come to show off because He was the Son of God. No, He came to show us what is possible through a surrendered life and to walk the life He walked and do the things that He did! He defeated the devil and gave us the empowerment of the resurrected life so that we can raise others up who are spiritually dead in His Name.

He gave us the power to "Heal the sick, cleanse the lepers, raise the dead, and cast out devils" (Matthew 10:8). Opening the eyes of the blind and the ears of the deaf are within the scope of the authority we have been given. Oh, how it must grieve His heart when people live a half-hearted and powerless Christian life, thinking their salvation is for themselves only. The lengths God went to in order to show us our value to Him and empower us to destroy the works of the enemy is amazing! Not only did Jesus die to have our sins forgiven but He rose again to show us the pathway to the resurrected life that overcomes the world. This is the full gospel message, and it should fill us with the Spirit of the risen Savior to the degree that we desire only to see His glory manifest on this earth and in the lives of countless others.

We are witnesses who testify to the power of the gospel, not only to save but to establish in ourselves a righteous overcoming life. We demonstrate the power of the resurrection every time we give our testimony, and we affect the lives of others by how we live and what we carry in our hearts. We are commissioned ambassadors for the kingdom of God. We have been given authority to carry out His plans here on earth.

The power of the resurrected life is supernatural. It forces every adversity to bow the knee. Even death itself no longer has the power to hold us captive. Our minds are set on the eternal things of God and the promise of life everlasting in the hereafter where we will live forever with our Lord and Savior and be reunited with those whom we love.

We can go through our lives trying to fill our hearts and feed our desires with things of this world, yet they are, at best, brief and fleeting. We end up chasing the things of this world instead of the Creator of all things. Our souls can never experience joy and contentment but will always strive for bigger, better, and more. I love the verse in Proverbs 10:22 which says, "The blessing of the Lord makes a man rich and He adds no sorrow to it."

Take a moment to contemplate this question. Do you own your time, or is it owned by your home, your car payments, your loans, the banks or the things your heart pursues? Are you in servitude to the pursuit of the material things in life? Are you striving to climb your way up the corporate ladder of success? Is your focus on the things of this world rather than the things of God?

This can happen and does happen to many. Before you know it, life becomes Jesus-incorporated instead of Jesus-centered. Matthew 6:33 tells us, "But seek ye first the kingdom of God, and His righteousness and all these things will be added to you." Many of us live as if that verse says, "Seek ye first the things that you need to be comfortable in this world, and then add Jesus to it."

We go after material gain with all the fervor we can muster and burn ourselves out trying to achieve and accomplish our own objectives. Then we add God to it as if He were part of the reason we are pursuing all these things. When we stand before God, do we think He is going to be impressed with the size of our bank account or our earthly successes?

If He was not the center of why you were blessed, then you really need to examine your motives and have a come-to-Jesus moment. Mark 8:36 directly challenges the accomplishment-oriented approach to life. It asks, "What does it profit a man to gain the whole world and lose his own soul?"

Is it pride, greed, lust, envy, gluttony, wrath or vanity? These are known as the deadly sins that can ensnare the human heart and take us off the course of God's intentions for our blessings. David learned how to allow God to keep Him in check with his motives when He wrote Psalm 139:23-24 "Search me, O God, and know my heart: Search me, and see if there be any wicked way in me." He was in a deep love relationship with God that allowed everything He did to be processed in tandem with God's intentions and desires for his life.

Was David a perfect man? By no means, but he was a man after God's own heart and did not want to lose the love of God over his life. He realized that everything he was able to do and everything he accomplished was an outcome of the intimate relationship he had with his Creator. When He sinned, he repented with heartfelt sorrow. When He triumphed, he exalted the Lord as the source of his strength!

While we can glean much from David's example, ultimately, the perfect example was Jesus. He never had to repent, and He showed us that obedience is far better than repentance. He was the model of a life that is perfectly yielded to God's will and that produces fruit for His glory. We have been redeemed so that we can learn to walk in that supernatural anointing. In this journey, we first commit ourselves to the process of sanctification and yield to the transforming renewal of our hearts and minds. We are not automatically sinless by way of accepting the Lord, but we become God-conscious. In that process, we sin less. We are constantly in the process of being renewed in the spirit of our minds. Gradually, the things that used to so easily ensnare us begin to lose their power over us and we develop a hunger and a thirst for the righteousness of God.

Look at some of the characters in the Bible that God used to advance His kingdom. Peter was an angry and probably drunken fisherman when Jesus called him. Matthew was a tax collector and despised by most everyone that had to pay Roman taxes. David was a shepherd and Moses was a murderer who spoke with a stutter. Jonah was a coward that God had to put in the belly of a whale to get his attention and call him to obedience. These were not those whom the world would see as men who were qualified to do great things for God, but they were vessels chosen by God for His purposes. Did they sometimes need a little nudging? Did they always obey? Absolutely not! But they were chosen by God for purposes that mankind had no say in. It is God who raises men up and it is God who brings them low.

Are you qualified for service to your Creator? If you are doubting your worthiness, then join a long line of the lost and broken men and women that were used mightily by God. If you remember correctly, God changed the names of some of His elect. He changed Abram's name to Abraham and changed Jacob's name to Israel. When God changed their identity, the world looked at them differently and they became the renowned men of God and the patriarchs of faith that are revered throughout the annals of history and the Bible. They model what relentless faith looks like. They show us what rebounding from failures looks like and demonstrate how God can use flawed men to do great things. Never doubt your qualification to be used by God. Desire to be used by Him and He will honor your request regardless of past failures or self-driven accomplishments.

2 Chronicles 16:9 says, "For the eyes of the Lord run to and fro throughout the whole earth, to show Himself strong on the behalf of those whose hearts are perfect toward Him." Does this mean that we have to be perfect for His eyes to notice and choose us? No, but it does mean that we have to acknowledge our weakness and the fact that we have fallen short of His glory. We must approach Him from the posture of a yielded heart.

God said to Paul, "My grace is sufficient for you, for my power is made perfect in weakness" (2 Corinthians 12:8). Likewise, until we realize our desperate need of the salvation Jesus bought for us, we will not give God His rightful place upon the throne of our lives. He cannot use a self-centered heart to accomplish His purposes.

Why am I pointing to Jesus as the entire focus of this writing? It is because we all need to have "A Raptured Heart!" We all need to have a divinely inspired purpose attached to our reason for living. Without it we become like Solomon. As he pursued the desires of his flesh, he deviated from the desires of his Creator. "Meaningless, meaningless! Like chasing after the wind," were the words Solomon used to describe where his carnal life left him. The same will happen to us if we don't ground ourselves in a greater purpose and plan than the fulfillment of our own desires. We will realize, at the end, that life had no meaning or purpose.

We should live to hear the applause of our Savior and reject the applause of men. We do everything to glorify Him and in turn, we are blessed to be part of His great plan of salvation. He provides everything we need according to His riches in glory. God is not on a budget! He owns everything, including the air you just breathed. Our lives are a gift from Him not to be squandered or used to make the lives of others grievous for our own selfish gain.

When we partner with God in the purposes for our lives, we become part of God's plan for the salvation of the world. We become God focused and not self-focused. It is in this posture that we are fulfilled in every area of life. We end up blessed and not stressed. He fuels our ambitions. The world's false hope of more is always better loses its luster. We live life satisfied and feel loved and comforted by the goodness of God. Our finances, our future, our families and the passing of the blessings of God to the next generations are all part of this love relationship which envelopes the life of "A Raptured Heart."

We were rescued from the fiery pits of hell and damnation and released into the beauty and glorious love of His family and His favor! That is a reason to be really excited—like, off the charts excited! Ecstatic! Elated! Enamored! Overwhelmed by love and eager to respond with fervor and experience the fullness of the resurrected life. Don't ever doubt your value to God. Jesus died to show you how much you were valued. He died for your sins, but rose again for your justification!

Embrace the fact that Christ died to save us, and He resurrected to redeem us back to God. Your salvation is a huge display of God's mercy, but your restoration is for the purpose of bringing glory to the One who redeemed you. Jesus came to restore the glory of God to humanity. How can we reject such a magnificent and wonderful gift? Why would anyone even want to?

The enemy is holding some of God's children hostage to his lies, so go and set them free by the power of your raptured heart and the authority that Jesus has given you. Take a bold stand for Christ and draw a line in the sand with the enemy. Take back territory that was stolen in the lives of those who are feeling defeated. Share the testimony of how God redeemed your life and boldly proclaim freedom for the captives as your King and risen Savior proclaimed in Isaiah 61:1. "He came to heal the broken hearted, to proclaim liberty to captives and to open prison doors for those who are bound."

Become the fulfillment of what He died to give you and take a stand for the principles that He endowed you with. Live a lifestyle that carries the hallmarks of His majesty and His sovereignty in everything you do and everything you pursue Lift a standard against the enemy and proclaim the freedom of the Gospel to everyone you meet. Press on toward the high calling that you have been given in Christ Jesus and commit yourself to the works of A Raptured Heart.

Dear reader, I issue you a challenge to believe deeper than you have ever believed before and step out on the water with your Savior where the signs, wonders and miracles exist. They are there for those with the courage and boldness to step out of their comfort zone and take a leap of faith. Embrace the impossible because with God, "All things are possible through Christ who gives us strength" (Philippians 4:13).

CONCLUSION

Ongoing Glory

As I write this conclusion, I have just received the news that my dear brother and precious friend who led me to the Lord so many years ago in that prison cell, Al Huber, passed on to glory. If it were not for this man's labor in the Lord, this book probably would have never been written and this story would have never been told. How often do we plant seeds in the lives of others and never really witness the full extent of what God did with those seeds? I honestly believe that we will see the fullness of that harvest when we get to heaven. Knowing that someone is there because of you will be part of your reward. Al, may you be at peace and rest in the loving arms of our Lord and Savior Jesus Christ.

I continue full time as the Director of Discipleship at The Potter's House Ministry. I am blessed to have reconnected with another dear friend and powerful influence in my life, Pastor Ron Buch, who was a chaplain on work release when I was in Lancaster County Prison so many years ago. Mary Sanchez Buch and Ron Buch are the pastors at Breakout Ministries in Leola, Pennsylvania. I am very blessed to call them dear friends. We recently sat down and had a conversation as to what more we can do to create an impact on the lost in our communities and bring them the love of Christ.

Pastor Ron had a conversation with me as to how we could partner in creating a group and ministry directly focused on ministering to the recovering community. This led to the Jesus Advantage (JA) recovery ministry birthed out of a Christ-breathed passion that we share to set the captives free. Many have come to experience the love and grace and mercy of the Lord Jesus Christ and have bowed their knees at the feet of Jesus through this endeavor. Through a vale of tears, they come to discover their new, born-again identity and are set free by the power of the resurrected life. We have been privileged to baptize several of our attendees at The Potter's House of Still Waters campus in Brownstown, and many are seeking church membership as a result. I am seeing the fulfillment of all that God had shown me He wanted to do so many years ago in that prison cell. I just needed to yield my heart and my life to His plans and purposes for my life.

Mere words can never describe fully the extent of the impact that a life redeemed can have on an entire community. I invite and challenge you to look deeply into your own heart and life and ask yourselves this question: "What am I living for?" "How can I make a difference in the world around me and lead others to Christ and an eternal place of peace and rest for their weary souls?"

Everyone who embraces the call of God will find the true meaning in being a game changer in their own lives and live to fulfill the destiny to which God has called them. I invite you to join me in the greatest quest a human life can undertake in the search for true meaning and purpose in life. Take your place among God's elect for the salvation of others as you discover the true meaning of being "A Raptured Heart."

In the Service of His Kingdom,

Robert M. Weatherholtz

Contact Information

For more information or speaking engagements
contact Rob Weatherholtz at
PO Box 273
Brownstown, PA 17508
Rob@arapturedheart.com

Made in USA - Crawfordsville, IN
10090_9780578346700
02.18.2022 0930